=== THE ===
BIG BOOK
OF
Pizza

HEARST
HOME

Food Network Magazine

Editorial Director Maile Carpenter
Creative Director Deirdre Koribanick
Executive Director Liz Sgroi
Executive Managing Editor Robb Riedel
Executive Editor Ellen Seidman
Photo Director Alice Albert
Special Projects Editor Pamela Mitchell
Book Designer Rachel Keaveny

EDITORIAL
Deputy Food Editor Teri Tsang Barrett
Associate Editors Belle Bakst, Kelsey Hurwitz
Assistant Editor Lavanya Narayanan
Editorial Assistant Carol Lee

ART AND PHOTOGRAPHY
Deputy Art Director Lou DiLorenzo
Associate Photo Editor Kristen Hazzard
Photo Assistant Yasmeen Yuna Bae
Digital Imaging Specialist Matthew Montesano

COPY
Copy & Research Chief Chris Jagger
Research Chief Katherine Wessling
Deputy Managing Editor Sarah Esgro
Copy Editor David Cobb Craig
Editorial Business Manager Mariah Schlossmann

FOOD NETWORK KITCHEN
Test Kitchen Director Stephen Jackson
Recipe Developers Melissa Gaman, Khalil Hymore, Amy Stevenson
Recipe Tester Jessica D'Ambrosio

10TEN MEDIA, LLC
Managing Editor Vickie An
Creative Director Ian Knowles
Executive Editors Bob Der, Scott Gramling
Art Director Christian Rodriguez
Copy Editor Amy Ciauro Stellabotte

HEARST SPECIALS
Vice President & Publisher Jacqueline Deval
Group Creative Director Zachariah Mattheus
Deputy Director Nicole Fisher
Marketing & Sales Coordinator Nicole Plonski

HEARST MAGAZINE MEDIA, INC.
President Debi Chirichella
Global Chief Revenue Officer Lisa Ryan Howard
Chief Content Officer Kate Lewis
Chief Financial & Strategy Officer; Treasurer Regina Buckley
Senior Vice President, Consumer Revenue & Development Brian Madden
President, Hearst Magazines International Jonathan Wright
Secretary Catherine A. Bostron

Publishing Consultants Gilbert C. Maurer, Mark F. Miller

HEARST
President & Chief Executive Officer Steven R. Swartz
Chairman William R. Hearst III
Executive Vice Chairman Frank A. Bennack, Jr.
Chief Operating Officer Mark E. Aldam

WARNER BROS. DISCOVERY
Chairman & Chief Content Officer, US Networks Group Kathleen Finch
Chief Marketing Officer, US Networks Karen Bronzo

HEARST HOME

Book design by Rachel Keaveny.
Library of Congress Cataloging-in-Publication Data is available.

10 9 8 7 6 5 4 3 2 1

Published by Hearst Home, an imprint of
Hearst Books/Hearst Communications, Inc.
300 West 57th Street
New York, NY 10019

For information about custom editions, special sales, premium and corporate purchases: hearst.com/magazines/hearst-books

Printed in China.

ISBN 978-1-950785-97-1

This is a book for pizza lovers, and we mean all of you: the diehards and the dabblers, the purists and the adventurers, the dough makers and the shortcut takers. We've been creating pizzas in Food Network's test kitchen for more than 15 years, and you're holding a book of our favorite recipes, from the simplest traditional pies to the most outrageous, unforgettable ones. We know many of you have a strong pizza POV, and we are here for you with foolproof doughs and tips for whatever form you endorse: Neapolitan, New York, Detroit, Chicago, thin crust, thick crust and all the pies in between. You'll find dozens of options ahead, so jump in. Pizza night will never be the same again!

Maile Carpenter
Editorial Director

Liz Sgroi
Executive Director

Cacio e Pepe Pizza with Ricotta
page 52

Contents

The Basics 14

Simple Pizzas 19

Specialty Pizzas 51

Pan Pizzas 85

Grilled Pizzas 113

Alternative Pizzas 133

Simple Pizzas

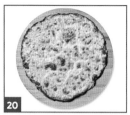

Basic Thin-Crust Pizzas

Neapolitan Pizzas

Margherita Pizzas

Hawaiian Pizza with Grilled Pineapple

Basic Pizzas with Homemade Sauce

Thin-Crust Veggie Pizzas

Sausage and Broccolini Pizza

Barbecue Chicken Pizza

White Clam Pizza

New York–Style Pizza

Three-Cheese White Pizzas

Individual Mushroom Pizzas with Arugula

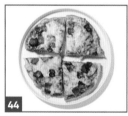

Three-Cheese Bacon Pizzas

Meatball Pizza

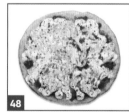

Spicy Margherita Pizzas

Specialty Pizzas

52 Cacio e Pepe Pizza with Ricotta

54 Butternut Squash–Soppressata Pizza

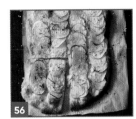
56 Potato-Rosemary Pizza

58 Cauliflower, Tomato and Olive Pizza

60 Brussels Sprouts–Pancetta Pizza

61 Mini Bacon-and-Egg Pizzas

62 Arugula-Prosciutto Pizza

64 Pizza with Clams and Broccoli Rabe

66 Potato and Bacon Pizza

68 Sausage Pizza with Arugula and Grapes

70 Quattro Stagioni Pizzas

72 Barbecue Mushroom Pizza

74 Sausage Pizza with Spinach Salad

76 Everything Bagel Pizza

78 Taco Pizza

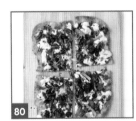
80 White Pizza with Broccolini

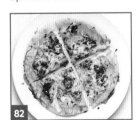
82 Corned Beef and Cabbage Pizzas

Pan Pizzas

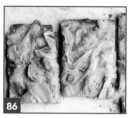

86
Sheet-Pan Pizza with Potatoes and Fennel

88
Basic Sicilian Pizza

90
Sicilian Pizza with Sausage and Peppers

92
Sheet-Pan Pizza alla Vodka

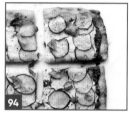

94
Sheet-Pan Pizza with Arugula Pesto

96
Skillet Taco Pizza

98
Deep-Dish Pizza with Spicy Sausage and Olives

100
Basic Deep-Dish Pizzas

102
Deep-Dish Pepperoni Pizza with Pepperoncini

104
Sheet-Pan Pepperoni Pizza with Hot Honey

106
Sheet-Pan Hawaiian Pizza

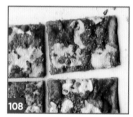

108
Sheet-Pan Pizza with Roasted Red Peppers

110
Sheet-Pan Spinach Pizza with Sesame Seeds

Grilled Pizzas

114
Grilled White Pizza with Fennel Salad

116
Grilled Pizza alla Vodka

117
Grilled Pizza with Spinach and Kale

118
Grilled Pizza with Pork and Pineapple

120
Grilled Pizza with Mushrooms and Fontina

121
Grilled Pizza with Hummus and Tomatoes

122
Grilled Pizza with Shrimp and Feta

124
Grilled Pizza with Spicy Chorizo and Corn

125
Grilled White Pizza with Garlic

126
Grilled Pizza with Summer Squash

128
Grilled Pizza with Peaches and Burrata

129
Grilled Ranch Pizza with Bacon and Broccoli

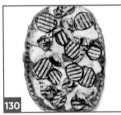
130
Grilled Pizza with Eggplant and Artichokes

Alternative Pizzas

134 Tahini-Carrot Puff Pastry Pizza

136 Ham and Cheese Pie with Artichokes and Broccoli

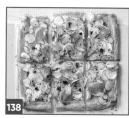
138 Smoked Salmon Puff Pastry Pizza

140 Lavash Pizzas with Arugula and Prosciutto

142 Bacon-and-Egg Puff Pastry Pizzas

144 Tortilla Pizzas with Chorizo

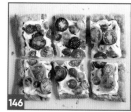
146 Heirloom Tomato Puff Pastry Pizza

148 Cauliflower-Crust Pizza with Mushrooms

150 Jalapeño Popper Tortilla Pizzas

152 Asparagus-Beet Puff Pastry Pizza

154 Cauliflower-Crust Pizzas with Artichokes

156 Grilled Pita Pizzas with Tomatoes and Arugula

158 Pepperoni Pizzagna

160 Barbecue Sausage French Bread Pizzas

162 Spinach-Artichoke Pizza Bagels

164 Philly Cheesesteak Pita Pizzas

166 Beet and Onion Pie

168 Artichoke French Bread Pizzas

169 Naan Pizzas with Tandoori Chicken

170 Beef Pita Pizzas

The Basics

Here's everything you need to get started: a foolproof dough recipe, plus tips for toppings, tools and more.

All-Purpose Pizza Dough

ACTIVE: 20 min **I** TOTAL: 1 hr 50 min **I** MAKES: 2 pounds

1½ teaspoons active dry yeast
1½ cups warm water (100° to 110°)
2 cups bread flour
1¾ cups all-purpose flour, plus more for dusting
2 teaspoons sugar
2 teaspoons kosher salt
2 tablespoons extra-virgin olive oil,
   plus more for the bowl

The dough should look shaggy before you knead it.

1. Sprinkle the yeast over the warm water in a small bowl. Let stand until dissolved and slightly foamy, 5 to 10 minutes.

2. Meanwhile, whisk the bread flour, all-purpose flour, sugar and salt in a large bowl and make a well in the center. Pour the yeast mixture into the well and add the olive oil. Stir with a wooden spoon until a shaggy dough forms.

3. Turn out the dough onto a lightly floured surface. Dust the dough with flour and knead, dusting with more flour as needed, until it's smooth and elastic but still slightly tacky, 3 to 5 minutes.

4. Transfer the dough to an oiled bowl, turning to coat. Cover with plastic wrap and let rise in a warm place until doubled in size, about 1½ hours. Divide the dough into two 1-pound balls. If you aren't using the dough right away, wrap it in plastic wrap and refrigerate for up to 2 days or freeze for up to 3 months. Bring to room temperature before using.

THE GOLDEN RULES
OF HOMEMADE PIZZA DOUGH

Make sure your water is hot enough to activate the yeast. It should be between 100° and 110°. If the yeast doesn't get foamy or frothy, start over with new yeast.	Measure the flour by spooning it into your measuring cup, then leveling it off with a knife. Never pack the flour; you'll end up adding too much.	Knead the dough until it's smooth and elastic. Follow the times in the recipe—it's possible to overwork it.	If you refrigerate your dough, be sure to bring it to room temperature before using it. Cold dough is hard to stretch and can easily tear.	Unless otherwise directed, stretch pizza dough with your hands, not a rolling pin— you don't want to press out the air pockets.

15

All-Purpose Pizza Sauce

ACTIVE: 10 min **|** TOTAL: 10 min
MAKES: about 1½ cups

1   15-ounce can crushed
    tomatoes
1   clove garlic, grated
1   teaspoon extra-virgin olive oil
¼   teaspoon dried oregano
Pinch of sugar, plus more to taste
Kosher salt and freshly
    ground pepper

1. Combine the tomatoes, garlic and olive oil in a large bowl.

2. Add the oregano and sugar; season with salt and pepper. Add more sugar, if needed.

Topping Tips

Watch out for toppings that contain a lot of moisture, like fresh tomatoes or raw mushrooms. They can make your crust soggy.

For a stretchy cheese pull, go with low-moisture mozzarella. Fresh mozzarella contains more water, so it's best used in combination with another cheese.

When making deep-dish pizza, put a layer of cheese on first, then add the sauce and other toppings. The cheese seals the crust and prevents sogginess.

Add herbs or other fresh toppings after the pie comes out of the oven. A drizzle of olive oil is never a bad idea either!

TOOLS OF THE TRADE

PIZZA PEEL
Slide your pizza in and out of the oven with a peel. If you don't have one, use an upside-down baking sheet.

PIZZA WHEEL
You can cut pizza with a chef's knife (or even kitchen shears!), but a pizza wheel is much easier.

PIZZA STONE
Bake your pizza directly on a stone—it gets super hot and helps crisp up the crust. Preheat the stone for at least an hour for the best results.

SHEET PAN
You'll need a sturdy rimmed baking sheet for sheet-pan pizzas.

BAKING STEEL
This heavy slab of pure steel is an alternative to a stone. Preheat it the same way, but beware: It can cook pizza faster than a stone.

NO PIZZA STONE? NO PROBLEM!
A stone or steel is a great investment for pizza makers, but if you don't have one, just use a baking sheet instead. Put an upside-down baking sheet on the bottom oven rack and preheat it. When it's time to bake, slide your pizza directly onto the hot baking sheet—the crust will get nice and crisp.

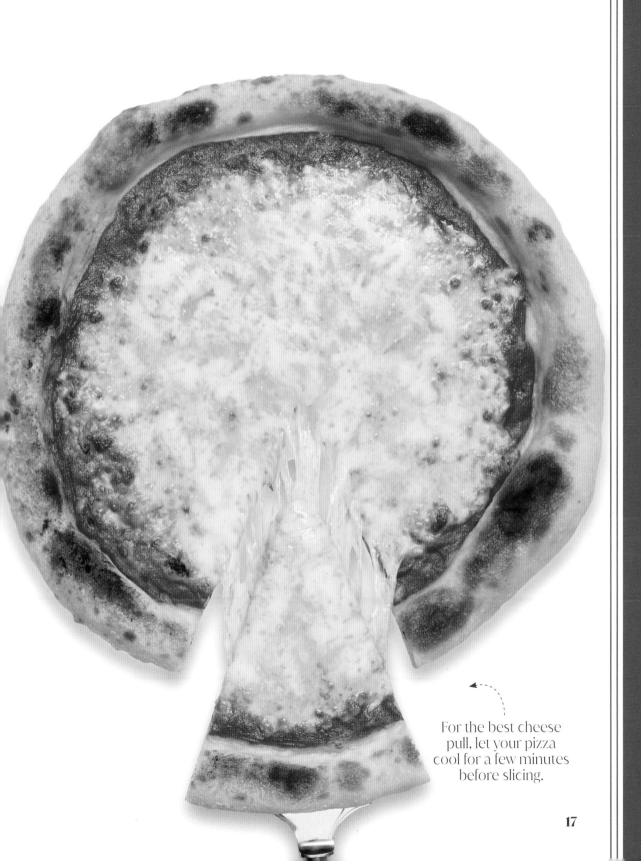

For the best cheese
pull, let your pizza
cool for a few minutes
before slicing.

Margherita
Pizza
page 25

Simple PIZZAS

———

These are the classic, no-fuss pies you know and love from your favorite pizzeria. Now you can make them at home!

The toppings go all the way to the edge on this pie.

Basic Thin-Crust Pizzas

ACTIVE: 1 hr 20 min ❙ TOTAL: 1½ hr (plus 1½ hr rising) ❙ SERVES: 6 to 8

FOR THE DOUGH

1½ teaspoons active dry yeast
1½ cups warm water
     (100° to 110°)
2   cups bread flour
1¾ cups all-purpose flour,
     plus more for dusting
2   teaspoons sugar
2   teaspoons kosher salt
2   tablespoons extra-virgin
     olive oil, plus more for
     the bowl

FOR THE PIZZAS

½   cup pizza sauce
¼   cup grated parmesan
     cheese
2½ cups grated low-moisture
     mozzarella cheese

1. Make the dough: Sprinkle the yeast over the warm water in a small bowl. Let stand until dissolved and slightly foamy, 5 to 10 minutes. Meanwhile, whisk the bread flour, all-purpose flour, sugar and salt in a large bowl and make a well in the center. Pour the yeast mixture into the well and add the olive oil. Stir with a wooden spoon until a shaggy dough forms. Turn out the dough onto a lightly floured surface, dust the dough with flour and knead, dusting with more flour as needed, until very smooth and elastic but still slightly tacky, 3 to 5 minutes.

2. Transfer the dough to an oiled bowl, turning to coat. Cover with plastic wrap and let rise in a warm place until doubled in size, about 1½ hours. Meanwhile, preheat the oven to 500° (use the convection setting, if available) with a pizza stone or inverted large baking sheet in the lower third of the oven.

3. Divide the dough into 2 balls. (You will need only 1 ball of dough for these pizzas; refrigerate or freeze the other ball of dough for another use.) On a lightly floured surface, cut the remaining ball of dough in half. Roll out 1 piece of dough on a lightly floured piece of parchment paper into a thin 12-inch round with a rolling pin (keep the other piece of dough covered).

4. Make the pizzas: Spread half of the pizza sauce on the dough round, going all the way to the edge. Sprinkle with half of the parmesan. Transfer the pizza (on the parchment) to the hot stone and bake until the crust is set, 4 to 5 minutes.

5. Remove the pizza from the oven and top with half of the mozzarella, going all the way to the edge. Return the pizza to the stone, then slide out the parchment from under it. Bake until the crust is golden brown and the cheese is melted, about 10 minutes. Repeat to make another pizza.

Neapolitan Pizzas

ACTIVE: 30 min I TOTAL: 2½ hr (plus overnight rising) I SERVES: 4 to 8

FOR THE DOUGH

- 1½ cups plus 2 tablespoons warm water (100° to 110°)
- ¾ teaspoon active dry yeast
- 4 cups unbleached all-purpose flour, plus more as needed
- 2½ teaspoons kosher salt
- Extra-virgin olive oil, for brushing

FOR THE PIZZAS

- 1 28-ounce can whole peeled San Marzano tomatoes
- Kosher salt
- Cornmeal, for dusting
- 8 ounces fresh mozzarella cheese, sliced
- Extra-virgin olive oil, for drizzling
- Torn fresh basil, for topping

1. Make the dough: Combine the warm water and yeast in a small bowl, stirring to dissolve the yeast. Combine the flour and salt in a medium bowl. Add the yeast mixture to the flour and stir to make a shaggy dough. (The dough should be tacky. If it feels too wet and sticky, add flour, 1 tablespoon at a time; if it's too stiff, add a little water.) Transfer to a lightly oiled surface and knead until smooth and elastic, about 3 minutes. Place an inverted bowl over the dough and let rise slightly, 30 minutes. Divide the dough into 4 pieces and form each into a ball; arrange 3 inches apart on a lightly oiled baking sheet. Brush the top of the dough lightly with olive oil and cover the baking sheet with plastic wrap. Refrigerate overnight.

2. Remove the dough from the refrigerator 2 hours before baking; let sit, covered, until ready to use. About 1 hour before baking, put a pizza stone or inverted baking sheet on the middle oven rack and preheat to 500° (or 550° if your oven goes that high).

3. Make the pizzas: Combine the tomatoes and their juices with 1 teaspoon salt in a blender; blend until smooth. Generously sprinkle a pizza peel or inverted baking sheet with cornmeal. Place 1 ball of dough upside down on the cornmeal using floured hands. Gently pull the dough into an 8- to 10-inch round, reflouring your hands as needed and being careful not to deflate the dough. Spread about ¼ cup tomato sauce on the crust; top with one-quarter of the mozzarella. Drizzle with 1 to 2 teaspoons olive oil and season with salt.

4. Slide the pizza onto the hot stone and bake until the crust is golden brown and the cheese is bubbling, 7 to 9 minutes. Transfer to a cutting board and sprinkle with basil. Let cool slightly. Repeat to make 3 more pizzas.

PRO TIPS

Use a good-quality unbleached flour for this delicate pizza dough. Bleaching weakens the gluten.

Be sure to refrigerate the dough overnight— that's what gives this crust a pillowy, slightly chewy texture.

Neapolitan pizza is known for its light, airy crust.

According to legend, margherita pizza was named after an Italian queen!

Margherita Pizzas

ACTIVE: 40 min I TOTAL: 1 hr (plus 1½ hr rising) I SERVES: 6

FOR THE DOUGH

3¾ cups all-purpose flour, plus more for dusting
1½ teaspoons fine salt
1⅓ cups warm water (100° to 110°)
1 tablespoon sugar
1 ¼-ounce packet active dry yeast
3 tablespoons extra-virgin olive oil, plus more for brushing

FOR THE PIZZAS

1 cup crushed San Marzano tomatoes
½ teaspoon dried oregano
Kosher salt and freshly ground pepper
Extra-virgin olive oil, for drizzling
½ pound mozzarella cheese, diced
Torn fresh basil, for topping

1. Make the dough: Whisk the flour and fine salt in a large bowl. Make a well in the middle and add the water, sugar and yeast; let sit until foamy, then mix in the olive oil. Stir the dry ingredients into the wet ingredients to make a shaggy dough. Turn out onto a floured surface and knead until the dough is smooth, about 5 minutes. Brush with more olive oil, transfer to a clean bowl, cover and let rise until doubled in size, about 1½ hours. Meanwhile, place a pizza stone or inverted baking sheet on the lowest oven rack and preheat to 500°.

2. Divide the dough into 2 balls. (You will need only 1 ball of dough for these pizzas; refrigerate or freeze the other ball of dough for another use.) Divide the remaining dough ball into 2 pieces. Stretch each piece into a thin 9-inch round on a floured pizza peel, large wooden cutting board or piece of parchment paper.

3. Make the pizzas: Spread the tomatoes on the dough. Top with the oregano, season with kosher salt and pepper and drizzle with olive oil. Slide the pizzas (on the parchment, if using) onto the hot stone. Bake until the crust is golden, about 15 minutes.

4. Sprinkle the pizzas with the mozzarella, basil, salt and pepper. Continue baking just until the cheese melts. Drizzle with more olive oil.

PRO TIPS

Margherita pizza is usually topped with crushed tomatoes instead of sauce. Use good-quality canned tomatoes.

Don't expect full cheesy coverage on a margherita: It's generally topped with pockets of diced or sliced mozzarella.

A drizzle of olive oil is the perfect final pizza topping—and it goes with every kind of pie! Drizzle right before serving.

Hawaiian Pizza with Grilled Pineapple

ACTIVE: 25 min **|** TOTAL: 40 min **|** SERVES: 4

1 pound pizza dough, at room temperature (see page 15 or use store-bought)

2 tablespoons extra-virgin olive oil

½ pineapple, peeled, cored and cut into rings

1 bunch scallions, white parts whole, green parts finely chopped

¼ cup barbecue sauce

1 tomato, diced

1 cup shredded pepper jack cheese (about 4 ounces)

½ cup shredded muenster cheese (about 2 ounces)

¼ pound deli-sliced ham, cut into large pieces

1. Put a pizza stone or inverted baking sheet in the oven and preheat to 475˚. Line another inverted baking sheet with parchment paper. Brush the pizza dough with the olive oil and center it on the parchment. Cover with another piece of parchment and set aside.

2. Heat a grill pan over medium-high heat. Grill the pineapple rings until marked, about 4 minutes per side. Transfer to a plate. Grill the scallion whites, turning, until charred, about 4 minutes. Transfer to the plate with the pineapple.

3. Combine the barbecue sauce and tomato in a small bowl. Stretch the pizza dough into a 10-by-14-inch rustic rectangle on the parchment; spread the barbecue sauce mixture on top. Sprinkle with the pepper jack and muenster cheeses and top with the grilled pineapple, ham and scallion whites and greens.

4. Slide the pizza (on the parchment) onto the hot stone. Bake until the cheese is bubbling and the crust is golden, about 15 minutes.

PRO TIPS

To peel a pineapple, slice off the top and bottom, then remove the peel with a chef's knife. Remove the "eyes" with a paring knife.

Barbecue sauce tastes great on this Hawaiian pizza, but you can use pizza sauce for a more traditional pie.

This is similar to a New York–style pizza. Not too thick, not too thin!

PRO TIPS

You can make the sauce ahead of time: It will keep in the refrigerator for up to 1 week or the freezer for up to 2 months.

For the best coverage, use shredded low-moisture mozzarella for this pizza. It gets extra stretchy—perfect for a cheese pull!

Basic Pizzas with Homemade Sauce

ACTIVE: 40 min I TOTAL: 40 min (plus 2 hr rising) I SERVES: 6

FOR THE DOUGH

- 2¾ cups all-purpose flour, plus more for dusting
- 1 tablespoon kosher salt
- 1 cup warm water (100° to 110°)
- 2 teaspoons sugar
- 1 teaspoon active dry yeast
- 2 tablespoons extra-virgin olive oil, plus more for the bowl

FOR THE PIZZAS

- 2 tablespoons extra-virgin olive oil
- 1 clove garlic, grated
- ¼ to ½ teaspoon red pepper flakes
- 1¾ cups tomato puree (preferably San Marzano)
- ½ teaspoon dried oregano
- Kosher salt
- 1 8-ounce bag shredded low-moisture mozzarella cheese (about 2 cups)

1. Make the dough: Combine the flour and salt in a large bowl. Make a well in the center and pour in the warm water. Sprinkle the sugar and yeast over the water and let stand until bubbling, 5 to 10 minutes. Pour the olive oil into the well, then stir with a wooden spoon to make a shaggy dough. Turn out onto a lightly floured surface and knead until smooth and elastic, about 1 minute. Place in a lightly oiled bowl, tightly cover with plastic wrap and let rise in a warm place until doubled in size, about 2 hours. About 1 hour before baking, put a pizza stone or inverted large baking sheet on the lowest oven rack and preheat to 500°.

2. Make the pizzas: Heat the olive oil in a medium saucepan over medium heat. Add the garlic and red pepper flakes and cook, stirring, until slightly softened, about 1 minute. Add the tomato puree and 2 cups water. Stir in the oregano and 1 teaspoon salt. Bring to a boil, then reduce the heat and simmer, stirring occasionally, until thickened, about 20 minutes.

3. Divide the dough into 2 balls. On a lightly floured surface, stretch 1 ball of dough into a 12- to 14-inch round. Transfer the dough to a piece of parchment paper, then slide the dough (on the parchment) onto a pizza peel or another inverted baking sheet.

4. Spread about ½ cup of the sauce on the crust in a thin layer, then scatter 1 cup mozzarella on top. Slide the pizza (on the parchment) onto the hot stone. Bake until the crust is golden brown and the cheese is bubbling, 8 to 10 minutes. Let cool 1 to 2 minutes before slicing. Repeat to make the second pizza.

Thin-Crust Veggie Pizzas

ACTIVE: 1 hr 20 min I TOTAL: 1½ hr (plus 1½ hr rising) I SERVES: 6 to 8

FOR THE DOUGH
1½ teaspoons active dry yeast
1½ cups warm water
(100° to 110°)
2 cups bread flour
1¾ cups all-purpose flour,
plus more for dusting
2 teaspoons sugar
2 teaspoons kosher salt
2 tablespoons extra-virgin
olive oil, plus more for
the bowl

FOR THE PIZZAS
1 small red bell pepper,
halved and seeded
8 ounces mixed mushrooms,
sliced
¼ cup extra-virgin olive oil,
plus more for drizzling
Kosher salt and freshly ground
pepper
2 onions, chopped
2 tablespoons tomato paste
1 teaspoon sugar, plus more
if needed
2 teaspoons balsamic vinegar
1 6-ounce jar marinated
artichoke hearts, drained
and chopped
¼ cup grated parmesan
cheese
⅔ cup ricotta cheese
Torn fresh basil, for topping

1. Make the dough: Sprinkle the yeast over the warm water in a small bowl. Let stand until dissolved and slightly foamy, 5 to 10 minutes. Meanwhile, whisk the bread flour, all-purpose flour, sugar and salt in a large bowl and make a well in the center. Pour the yeast mixture into the well and add the olive oil. Stir with a wooden spoon until a shaggy dough forms. Turn out the dough onto a lightly floured surface, dust the dough with flour and knead, dusting with more flour as needed, until very smooth and elastic but still slightly tacky, 3 to 5 minutes.

2. Transfer the dough to an oiled bowl, turning to coat. Cover with plastic wrap; let rise in a warm place until doubled in size, 1½ hours. Meanwhile, preheat the oven to 500° (use the convection setting, if available) with a pizza stone or inverted baking sheet in the lower third of the oven.

3. Make the pizzas: Line a rimmed baking sheet with foil; put the bell pepper halves on one side and the mushrooms on the other side. Drizzle with 2 tablespoons olive oil; toss to coat. Arrange the peppers cut-side down and roast, turning the peppers and stirring the mushrooms occasionally, until the vegetables are tender, 15 to 20 minutes; season with salt and pepper.

4. Meanwhile, heat the remaining 2 tablespoons olive oil in a medium nonstick skillet over medium heat. Add the onions, 1 teaspoon salt and a few grinds of pepper. Cook, stirring, until tender and lightly browned, 15 to 20 minutes, reducing the heat as needed. Stir in ¼ cup water, the tomato paste and sugar. Cook, stirring, until the tomato paste is a few shades darker, about 10 minutes. Remove from the heat and stir in the vinegar; season with salt, pepper and more sugar, if needed. Let cool.

5. Chop the roasted peppers. Transfer to a large bowl and stir in the mushrooms, artichoke hearts and a pinch each of salt and pepper.

6. Divide the dough into 2 balls. (You will need only 1 ball of dough for these pizzas; refrigerate or freeze the other ball of dough for another use.) On a floured surface, cut the remaining dough ball in half. Gently roll each piece into a small ball. Roll 1 piece of dough into a thin 12-inch round on a floured piece of parchment paper (keep the other piece of dough covered). Top the dough with half of the sauce, spreading it to the edge, then top with half of the vegetables and 2 tablespoons parmesan.

7. Transfer the pizza (on the parchment) to the hot stone and bake until the crust is set, 3 to 5 minutes. Slide out the parchment from under the pizza. Continue baking until the crust is golden brown and crisp, 7 to 10 more minutes. Remove the pizza to a cutting board and dot with half of the ricotta. Drizzle with olive oil, season with salt and top with basil. Repeat to make another pizza.

You'll get two thin-crust pizzas out of this recipe.

Sausage and Broccolini Pizza

ACTIVE: 25 min **I** TOTAL: 40 min **I** SERVES: 4

3	tablespoons extra-virgin olive oil
1	pound pizza dough, at room temperature (see page 15 or use store-bought)
1	14.5-ounce can diced tomatoes, drained
⅓	cup chopped fresh basil
⅔	cup ricotta cheese
2	cups shredded part-skim mozzarella cheese (about 8 ounces)
3	tablespoons chopped fresh mint

Kosher salt and freshly ground pepper

4	Italian sausages (about 12 ounces), casings removed
3	cloves garlic, thinly sliced
1	bunch broccolini, cut into florets

1. Put a pizza stone or inverted baking sheet on the lowest oven rack; preheat to 475°. Line another inverted baking sheet with parchment paper; drizzle with 2 tablespoons olive oil. Form the pizza dough into an 8-inch oval on the parchment; flip to coat with the oil. Drape with plastic wrap; set aside.

2. Combine the tomatoes and basil in a bowl. Mix the ricotta, mozzarella and mint in another bowl; season with ½ teaspoon salt and a few grinds of pepper.

3. Heat the remaining 1 tablespoon olive oil in a skillet over medium-high heat. Add the sausages and garlic; cook, breaking up the meat, until browned, about 5 minutes. Remove to a plate using a slotted spoon. Add the broccolini and ½ cup water to the drippings in the skillet and cook until tender, about 5 minutes.

4. Stretch the dough to 11 by 14 inches on the parchment; spoon the cheese mixture on top. Top with the tomatoes, sausage and broccolini. Slide the pizza (on the parchment) onto the hot stone. Bake until the crust is golden, about 15 minutes.

PRO TIPS

Canned diced tomatoes are very liquidy. Be sure to drain them before topping your pizza.

You can use hot or sweet Italian sausage for this pizza. If you're using links, remove the meat from the casings.

Barbecue Chicken Pizza

ACTIVE: 25 min **I** TOTAL: 40 min (plus 1½ hr rising) **I** SERVES: 4

FOR THE DOUGH

- 3¾ cups all-purpose flour, plus more for dusting
- 1½ teaspoons salt
- 1⅓ cups warm water (100° to 110°)
- 1 tablespoon sugar
- 1 ¼-ounce packet active dry yeast
- 3 tablespoons extra-virgin olive oil, plus more for brushing

FOR THE PIZZA

- ¼ cup barbecue sauce
- 1 cup shredded cooked chicken
- 3 scallions, thinly sliced
- 1 tablespoon pickled jalapeños
- 1 cup shredded cheddar cheese

1. Make the dough: Whisk the flour and salt in a large bowl. Make a well in the center and add the water, sugar and yeast; let sit until foamy, then mix in the olive oil. Stir the dry ingredients into the wet ingredients to make a shaggy dough. Turn out onto a floured surface and knead until the dough is smooth, about 5 minutes. Brush with more olive oil, then transfer to a clean bowl, cover and let rise until doubled in size, about 1½ hours. Meanwhile, place a pizza stone or inverted baking sheet on the lowest oven rack and preheat to 500°.

2. Divide the dough into 2 balls. (You will need only 1 ball of dough for this recipe; refrigerate or freeze the other ball of dough for another use.) Stretch the remaining dough ball into a 9-by-15-inch rectangle on a floured pizza peel, large wooden cutting board or piece of parchment paper.

3. Make the pizza: Spread the barbecue sauce on the dough. Top with the chicken, scallions, pickled jalapeños and cheddar. Slide the pizza (on the parchment, if using) onto the hot stone. Bake until the crust is golden, about 15 minutes.

PRO TIPS

Rotisserie chicken is the perfect shortcut for this pizza. You can also use leftover cooked chicken.

Pickled jalapeños are packed in a flavorful brine. Drain the brine into a separate container and use it to make salad dressing!

This is a take
on the beloved
New Haven
clam pie.

White Clam Pizza

ACTIVE: 20 min **|** TOTAL: 30 min **|** SERVES: 4

3 large cloves garlic, chopped
¼ cup extra-virgin olive oil, plus more for drizzling
1 pound pizza dough, at room temperature (see page 15 or use store-bought)
All-purpose flour, for kneading
Cornmeal, for dusting
Kosher salt
½ cup thinly sliced mozzarella cheese (about 4 ounces)
2 6.5-ounce cans chopped clams, juice drained and reserved
¼ teaspoon dried oregano
2 tablespoons grated parmesan cheese
2 cups baby arugula
Juice of 1 lemon
Red pepper flakes, for sprinkling

1. Place a pizza stone or inverted baking sheet on the lowest oven rack and preheat to 500˚.

2. Mix the garlic and olive oil in a small bowl. Knead the pizza dough about 6 times on a lightly floured surface. Roll and stretch into a 12-inch round. Place the dough on a pizza peel or another inverted baking sheet dusted with cornmeal.

3. Brush half of the garlic oil onto the dough; season with salt. Scatter the mozzarella and clams over the crust, then drizzle with 2 tablespoons of the reserved clam juice and the remaining garlic oil. Sprinkle with the oregano, parmesan, and salt to taste. Slide the pizza onto the hot stone. Bake until the crust is light brown, 13 to 15 minutes.

4. Just before the pizza is done, drizzle the arugula with olive oil and lemon juice. Pile on top of the pizza and sprinkle with red pepper flakes.

PRO TIPS

Don't toss the clam juice! The briny liquid adds extra flavor to this pizza.

Garlic oil is a simple way to dress up store-bought pizza dough: Brush it onto the crust before adding the toppings.

New York–Style Pizza

ACTIVE: 1 hr 20 min **|** TOTAL: 1½ hr (plus 1½ hr rising) **|** SERVES: 6 to 8

FOR THE DOUGH

- 1½ teaspoons active dry yeast
- 1½ cups warm water (100° to 110°)
- 2 cups bread flour
- 1¾ cups all-purpose flour, plus more for dusting
- 2 teaspoons sugar
- 2 teaspoons kosher salt
- 2 tablespoons extra-virgin olive oil, plus more for the bowl

Cornmeal, for dusting

FOR THE PIZZA

- ½ cup pizza sauce
- 2 tablespoons grated parmesan cheese
- 2 ounces torn fresh mozzarella cheese
- 1 heaping cup shredded low-moisture mozzarella cheese

1. Make the dough: Sprinkle the yeast over the warm water in a small bowl. Let stand until dissolved and foamy, 5 to 10 minutes. Meanwhile, whisk the bread flour, all-purpose flour, sugar and salt in a large bowl and make a well in the center. Pour the yeast mixture into the well and add the olive oil. Stir with a wooden spoon until a shaggy dough forms. Turn out the dough onto a lightly floured surface, dust the dough with flour and knead, dusting with more flour as needed, until very smooth and elastic but still slightly tacky, 3 to 5 minutes.

2. Transfer the dough to an oiled bowl, turning to coat. Cover with plastic wrap and let rise in a warm place until doubled in size, about 1½ hours. Meanwhile, preheat the oven to 500° (use the convection setting, if available) with a pizza stone, baking steel or inverted large baking sheet in the lower third of the oven.

3. Divide the dough into 2 balls. (You will need only 1 ball of dough for this pizza; refrigerate or freeze the other ball of dough for another use.) On a lightly floured surface or cornmeal-dusted piece of parchment paper, gently stretch and press the remaining dough ball into a 12- to 13-inch round.

4. Make the pizza: Spread the pizza sauce on the dough, leaving a ¾-inch border. Evenly top with the parmesan and two mozzarellas. Transfer the pizza (on the parchment) to the hot stone and bake until the crust is set, about 5 minutes. Slide out the parchment from under the pizza. Continue to bake until the crust is golden brown and the cheese is melted, 5 to 10 minutes.

PRO TIPS

Canned or jarred pizza sauce is fine for this pie, or you can make your own—find a recipe on page 16.

We used two types of mozzarella for this pizza: shredded low-moisture to cover the pie, then slices of fresh mozzarella for richness.

Cut this pie into big slices
then fold them in half to
eat them, like a true
New Yorker!

This one is for serious cheese lovers!

Three-Cheese White Pizzas

ACTIVE: 25 min **I** TOTAL : 45 min (plus 2 to 4 hr rising) **I** SERVES: 8

FOR THE DOUGH
1   teaspoon active dry yeast
1   cup warm water
    (100° to 110°)
2   teaspoons sugar
1   tablespoon extra-virgin olive
    oil, plus more for the bowls
3   cups all-purpose flour, plus
    more for dusting
2   teaspoons kosher salt

FOR THE PIZZAS
⅔   cup ricotta cheese
½   cup grated parmesan
    cheese (about 1 ounce)
¼   cup extra-virgin olive oil,
    plus more for brushing
2   cloves garlic, grated
½   teaspoon chopped fresh
    oregano or rosemary
¼ to ½ teaspoon red pepper
    flakes
Kosher salt
4   ounces fresh mozzarella
    cheese, thinly sliced

1. Make the dough: Combine the yeast, water and sugar in a food processor and pulse once to combine. Let sit until foamy, 5 to 10 minutes. Add the olive oil; pulse to combine. Mix the flour and salt in a medium bowl; add to the food processor and pulse until the dough pulls away from the side and gathers around the blade.

2. Turn out the dough onto a lightly floured surface and form into 2 even balls. Transfer to 2 lightly oiled bowls; cover with plastic wrap and let rise in a warm place until doubled in size, 2 to 4 hours. About 1 hour before baking, set a pizza stone or inverted large baking sheet on the lowest oven rack and preheat to 500°.

3. Make the pizzas: Combine the ricotta, parmesan, olive oil, garlic, oregano and red pepper flakes in a medium bowl; season with salt. Mix well.

4. Stretch 1 ball of dough into a 12-inch round on a lightly floured pizza peel or another inverted baking sheet. Spread half of the ricotta mixture on top, leaving a ½-inch border. Top with half of the mozzarella, then brush the edge of the dough lightly with olive oil.

5. Slide the pizza onto the hot stone and bake until the crust is golden and the cheese is bubbling, 7 to 10 minutes. Transfer to a cutting board and let cool slightly. Repeat to make the second pizza.

Individual Mushroom Pizzas with Arugula

ACTIVE: 30 min **I** TOTAL: 40 min **I** SERVES: 4

3 tablespoons extra-virgin olive oil, plus more for drizzling

1¼ pounds sliced mixed mushrooms

Kosher salt and freshly ground pepper

1 pound pizza dough, at room temperature (see page 15 or use store-bought)

2 cups shredded mozzarella cheese (about 8 ounces)

3 cloves garlic, minced

¼ cup chopped fresh parsley

Grated parmesan cheese, for topping

2 cups baby arugula

1 endive, chopped

½ small head radicchio, chopped

2 teaspoons white balsamic vinegar

1. Place an inverted baking sheet in the middle of the oven and another in the lower third; preheat to 500˚. Heat 2 tablespoons olive oil in a large nonstick skillet over high heat. Add the mushrooms and season with ½ teaspoon salt and a few grinds of pepper. Cook, stirring occasionally, until the mushrooms are browned and tender, 8 to 10 minutes. Remove from the heat.

2. Meanwhile, cut the pizza dough into 4 pieces. Drizzle each with olive oil and lightly rub. Place 2 pieces on a sheet of parchment paper and stretch each into a 6- to 8-inch round. Repeat with the remaining 2 pieces of dough. Sprinkle with the mozzarella, then top with the mushrooms and garlic. Transfer the pizzas (on the parchment) to a pizza peel or another inverted baking sheet, then slide onto the hot baking sheets. Bake until the crusts are golden and the cheese is bubbling, 12 to 15 minutes. Sprinkle with the parsley and parmesan.

3. Combine the arugula, endive and radicchio in a medium bowl. Drizzle with the vinegar and remaining 1 tablespoon olive oil; season with salt and pepper and toss. Top the pizzas with the salad.

PRO TIPS

You won't be able to fit all four of these individual pies on one pizza stone. Bake them on two inverted baking sheets instead.

If you like a traditional mushroom pie, just serve the salad on the side!

Try a new twist on the usual mushroom pizza.

A little bacon goes
a long way!

Three-Cheese Bacon Pizzas

ACTIVE: 25 min **I** TOTAL: 40 min **I** SERVES: 4

1   pound pizza dough, at room temperature (see page 15 or use store-bought)
All-purpose flour, for dusting
4   slices bacon, chopped
1   8-ounce can tomato sauce
2   tablespoons extra-virgin olive oil
1   clove garlic, grated
¼   teaspoon dried oregano
Kosher salt and freshly ground pepper
1   cup shredded mozzarella cheese (about 4 ounces)
1   cup shredded white cheddar cheese (about 4 ounces)
1   tablespoon grated parmesan cheese

1. Put a pizza stone or inverted baking sheet on the lowest oven rack and preheat to 475˚. Meanwhile, roll out the pizza dough into a 9-inch round on a lightly floured surface. Lightly dust a pizza peel or another inverted baking sheet with flour; lay the dough round on top and set aside.

2. Cook the bacon in a large skillet over medium heat, stirring, until crisp, about 6 minutes. Remove with a slotted spoon and drain on paper towels. Combine the tomato sauce, olive oil, garlic and oregano in a medium bowl; season with salt and pepper.

3. Slide the dough directly onto the hot stone and bake until lightly golden and puffy, about 7 minutes. Remove from the oven and let cool slightly, then carefully slice the crust in half horizontally with a serrated knife to make 2 thin crusts.

4. Turn the crusts cut-side up. Spread with the sauce mixture, then top evenly with the mozzarella, cheddar and bacon. Slide the pizzas back onto the hot stone; bake until the cheese melts and the crust is golden, about 8 more minutes. Sprinkle with the parmesan.

PRO TIPS

We baked the crust without toppings, then split it like an English muffin into two crusts. Use a long serrated knife to get an even cut.

Doctor up canned tomato sauce for this pizza: Stir in olive oil, grated garlic and dried oregano for extra flavor.

Meatball Pizza

ACTIVE: 25 min | TOTAL: 40 min (plus 1½ hr rising) | SERVES: 4

FOR THE DOUGH
3¾ cups all-purpose flour, plus
    more for dusting
1½ teaspoons salt
1⅓ cups warm water
    (100° to 110°)
1 tablespoon sugar
1 ¼-ounce packet active
    dry yeast
3 tablespoons extra-virgin
    olive oil, plus more for
    brushing

FOR THE PIZZA
Extra-virgin olive oil, for brushing
    and drizzling
½ cup tomato sauce
6 ounces fresh mozzarella
    cheese
8 cooked meatballs, sliced
Grated pecorino cheese, for
    sprinkling
Torn fresh basil, for sprinkling

1. Make the dough: Whisk the flour and salt in a large bowl. Make a well in the middle and add the water, sugar and yeast; let sit until foamy, then mix in the olive oil. Stir the dry ingredients into the wet ingredients to make a shaggy dough. Turn out onto a floured surface and knead until the dough is smooth, about 5 minutes. Brush with more olive oil, transfer to a clean bowl, cover and let rise until doubled in size, about 1½ hours. Meanwhile, place a pizza stone or inverted baking sheet on the lowest oven rack and preheat to 500°.

2. Divide the dough into 2 balls. (You will need only 1 ball of dough for this pizza; refrigerate or freeze the other ball of dough for another use.) Press the remaining dough ball into a 15-inch round pizza pan.

3. Make the pizza: Brush the dough with olive oil, then spread with the tomato sauce. Top with the mozzarella. Place the pizza pan on the hot stone. Bake until the crust is just crisp, about 10 minutes.

4. Cover the pizza evenly with the meatballs; sprinkle with pecorino and basil. Drizzle with more olive oil. Bake until the pizza is browned, 5 to 7 minutes.

PRO TIPS

A pizza pan is ideal for this recipe—it's easier to take the pie in and out of the oven, considering the heavy meatball topping.

When baking pizza in a pan, you should still use a stone. It helps the pan get nice and hot and makes the crust crisp.

This is a great way to use up leftover meatballs!

Red pepper flakes give this pizza a kick.

Spicy Margherita Pizzas

ACTIVE: 25 min **I** TOTAL: 45 min (plus 2 to 4 hr rising) **I** SERVES: 8

FOR THE DOUGH
1	teaspoon active dry yeast
1	cup warm water (100° to 110°)
2	teaspoons sugar
1	tablespoon extra-virgin olive oil, plus more for the bowls
3	cups all-purpose flour, plus more for dusting
2	teaspoons kosher salt

FOR THE PIZZAS
1	14.5-ounce can whole peeled tomatoes, crushed by hand
2	tablespoons extra-virgin olive oil, plus more for brushing
1	clove garlic, grated
1	teaspoon red pepper flakes
	Kosher salt
6	ounces fresh mozzarella cheese, thinly sliced

1. Make the dough: Combine the yeast, water and sugar in a food processor and pulse once to combine. Let sit until foamy, 5 to 10 minutes. Add the olive oil and pulse to combine. Mix the flour and salt in a medium bowl; add to the food processor and pulse until the dough pulls away from the side and gathers around the blade.

2. Turn out the dough onto a lightly floured surface and form into 2 even balls. Transfer to 2 lightly oiled bowls; cover with plastic wrap and let rise in a warm place until doubled in size, 2 to 4 hours. About 1 hour before baking, set a pizza stone or inverted large baking sheet on the lowest oven rack and preheat to 500°.

3. Make the pizzas: Combine the tomatoes, olive oil, garlic, red pepper flakes and 1 teaspoon salt in a medium bowl. Mix well.

4. Stretch 1 ball of dough into a 12-inch round on a lightly floured pizza peel or another inverted baking sheet. Spread about ½ cup of the tomato mixture on the dough, leaving a ½-inch border. Top with half of the mozzarella, then brush the edge of the dough lightly with olive oil.

5. Slide the pizza onto the hot stone and bake until the crust is golden and the cheese is bubbling, 8 to 10 minutes. Transfer to a cutting board and let cool slightly. Repeat to make the second pizza.

PRO TIPS

Making this pizza dough is super easy with a food processor: Just pulse it to combine.

Pizza dough freezes well. Let it rise, then wrap it tightly in plastic wrap and freeze for up to 2 months. Bring it to room temperature before using.

Sausage
Pizza with
Arugula and
Grapes
page 68

Specialty PIZZAS

These unique pies are
all about the toppings.
Find your new favorite combo!

Cacio e Pepe Pizza with Ricotta

ACTIVE: 30 min **I** TOTAL: 45 min (plus 2 hr rising) **I** SERVES: 4

FOR THE DOUGH

- 2¾ cups all-purpose flour, plus more for dusting
- 1 tablespoon kosher salt
- 1 teaspoon coarsely ground pepper
- 1 cup warm water (100° to 110°)
- 2 teaspoons sugar
- 1 teaspoon active dry yeast
- 2 tablespoons extra-virgin olive oil, plus more for the bowl

FOR THE PIZZA

- ½ cup ice cubes
- ¼ cup extra-virgin olive oil
- 1 cup fresh ricotta cheese (about 8 ounces)
- 1 cup finely grated pecorino romano cheese (about 4 ounces)
- 2 teaspoons coarsely ground pepper

Kosher salt

1. Make the dough: Combine the flour, salt and pepper in a large bowl. Make a well in the center and pour in the warm water. Sprinkle the sugar and yeast over the water and let stand until bubbling, 5 to 10 minutes. Pour the olive oil into the well, then stir with a wooden spoon to make a shaggy dough. Turn out onto a lightly floured surface and knead until smooth and elastic, about 5 minutes. Place in a lightly oiled bowl, tightly cover with plastic wrap and let rise in a warm place until doubled in size, about 2 hours.

2. One hour before baking, put a pizza stone or inverted baking sheet in the lower third of the oven and preheat to 500°. On a lightly floured surface, stretch the dough into a 12-inch round.

3. Make the pizza: Transfer the dough to a well-floured pizza peel or another inverted baking sheet. Dot with the ice and drizzle with 2 tablespoons olive oil. Slide the pizza onto the hot stone. Bake until the crust is golden brown and the ice melts, 12 to 13 minutes.

4. Transfer the pizza to a cutting board and cover with small spoonfuls of the ricotta. Sprinkle with the pecorino and pepper; drizzle the remaining 2 tablespoons olive oil on top and season with salt.

PRO TIPS

Baking pizza dough with ice on top may sound strange, but it leaves the crust moist and starchy on top—a great base for all that cheese.

Use coarse freshly ground pepper for this pizza—it's a star ingredient (cacio e pepe is Italian for "cheese and pepper").

Top the crust with the cheese as soon as it comes out of the oven so it starts to melt a bit.

Butternut Squash–Soppressata Pizza

ACTIVE: 20 min **|** TOTAL: 35 min **|** SERVES: 4

½   small butternut squash, peeled, seeded and thinly sliced crosswise

1   tablespoon extra-virgin olive oil, plus more for drizzling

2   teaspoons honey

1   teaspoon balsamic vinegar

¼   teaspoon red pepper flakes

Kosher salt

1   pound pizza dough, at room temperature (see page 15 or use store-bought)

All-purpose flour, for dusting

12 to 16 sage leaves, torn

1½ cups shredded Italian cheese blend (about 6 ounces)

3   ounces thinly sliced soppressata

2   tablespoons roughly chopped fresh parsley

1. Position racks in the middle and lower third of the oven and put a pizza stone or inverted baking sheet on the middle rack; preheat to 475˚. Toss the squash, olive oil, honey, vinegar, red pepper flakes and ½ teaspoon salt on another baking sheet; spread in a single layer. Bake on the lower rack until the squash is lightly browned and tender, about 10 minutes.

2. Stretch the dough into a 12-by-16-inch rectangle on a floured surface; transfer to a piece of parchment paper. Top with the roasted squash, sage, cheese and soppressata. Slide the pizza (on the parchment) onto the hot stone. Bake until the cheese is bubbling and the crust is golden, 10 to 12 minutes. Transfer to a cutting board; top with the parsley and drizzle with olive oil.

PRO TIPS

Butternut squash skin is thick, but you can remove it with a good vegetable peeler. A Y-shaped peeler works best.

To remove parsley leaves from their stems, hold the bunch by the stems and run your knife down the length to shave off the leaves.

Potato-Rosemary Pizza

ACTIVE: 30 min **I** TOTAL: 45 min (plus 1½ hr rising) **I** SERVES: 4

FOR THE DOUGH

3¾ cups all-purpose flour, plus more for dusting

1½ teaspoons salt

1⅓ cups warm water (100° to 110°)

1 tablespoon sugar

1 ¼-ounce packet active dry yeast

3 tablespoons extra-virgin olive oil, plus more for brushing

FOR THE PIZZA

1 russet potato, thinly sliced crosswise

Extra-virgin olive oil, for drizzling

1 tablespoon chopped fresh rosemary

Flaky sea salt

Grated pecorino cheese, for topping

1. Make the dough: Whisk the flour and salt in a large bowl. Make a well in the middle and add the water, sugar and yeast to the well. Set aside until foamy, then add the olive oil and mix everything together. Knead until the dough is smooth, about 5 minutes. Brush a large bowl generously with olive oil and add the dough, turning to coat. Cover and let rise until doubled in size, about 1½ hours. Meanwhile, place a pizza stone or inverted baking sheet on the lowest oven rack and preheat to 500°.

2. Divide the dough into 2 balls. (You will need only 1 ball of dough for this pizza; refrigerate or freeze the other ball of dough for another use.) Stretch the remaining dough ball into a 9-by-15-inch rectangle on a floured pizza peel, large wooden cutting board or sheet of parchment paper.

3. Make the pizza: Cover the dough with the potato slices, leaving a 1-inch border. Drizzle with olive oil, then sprinkle with the rosemary and sea salt. Top with pecorino. Slide the pizza onto the hot stone and bake until the crust is golden, about 15 minutes.

PRO TIPS

Use a mandoline to slice the potato. You'll get nice thin slices that will cook quickly and evenly.

To strip rosemary leaves off their stems, pinch the top of a sprig, then run your fingers down the stem from top to bottom.

Kosher salt is great for seasoning, but flaky sea salt is better for finishing. It adds a great salty crunch.

Cauliflower, Tomato and Olive Pizza

ACTIVE: 30 min **I** TOTAL: 50 min **I** SERVES: 4 to 6

½ large head cauliflower, cut into small florets (about 4 cups)

7 tablespoons extra-virgin olive oil

¼ teaspoon red pepper flakes, plus more for topping

Kosher salt

2 cloves garlic, minced

1 14-ounce can whole peeled tomatoes, crushed by hand

½ cup fresh parsley, roughly chopped

⅓ cup pitted kalamata olives, roughly chopped

1 tablespoon capers, rinsed

Finely grated zest of 1 lemon, plus 2 teaspoons lemon juice

1 pound pizza dough, at room temperature (see page 15 or use store-bought)

4 ounces fresh mozzarella cheese, thinly sliced

½ cup grated parmesan cheese

1. Place a baking sheet in the upper third of the oven and a pizza stone or inverted baking sheet in the lower third; preheat to 475°. Toss the cauliflower with 2 tablespoons olive oil, the red pepper flakes and ¼ teaspoon salt in a medium bowl. Spread in a single layer on the top hot baking sheet. Roast until the cauliflower is golden brown on the bottom, 10 to 12 minutes.

2. Meanwhile, combine 1 tablespoon olive oil and the garlic in a medium saucepan over medium-high heat. Cook, stirring frequently, until the garlic just starts to turn golden, about 2 minutes. Add the tomatoes and ½ teaspoon salt and simmer until reduced to about 1 cup, about 8 minutes; let cool. Combine the parsley, olives, capers, lemon zest and juice, and 2 tablespoons olive oil in a medium bowl; set aside.

3. Brush a large piece of parchment paper with the remaining 2 tablespoons olive oil. Stretch the pizza dough into an 11-by-15-inch rectangle on the parchment. Transfer the dough (on the parchment) to a pizza peel or another inverted baking sheet. Spread the tomato sauce all over the dough, leaving a ½-inch border. Top with the mozzarella, then scatter the roasted cauliflower on top and sprinkle with the parmesan. Slide the pizza (on the parchment) onto the hot stone. Bake until the crust is golden, 20 to 25 minutes. Top with the parsley-olive mixture; sprinkle with red pepper flakes.

PRO TIPS

To pit olives easily, lay the flat side of a chef's knife on top of a few olives, then pound with your fist; the olives will split open.

This pizza tastes great with anchovies on top. Roughly chop a few oil-packed anchovies and sprinkle onto the pie just before serving.

PRO TIP

Pile on the brussels sprouts—they'll shrink a lot in the oven.

Brussels Sprouts–Pancetta Pizza

ACTIVE: 20 min ▍ TOTAL: 45 min ▍ SERVES: 4

All-purpose flour, for dusting
1   pound pizza dough, at room temperature (see page 15 or use store-bought)
Extra-virgin olive oil, for drizzling
1   clove garlic, grated
4   ounces taleggio cheese, sliced
8 to 10 brussels sprouts, thinly sliced
4   ounces diced pancetta
⅓   cup grated pecorino cheese
Red pepper flakes, for sprinkling
Kosher salt

1. Place a pizza stone or inverted baking sheet on the lowest oven rack; preheat to 500°.

2. On a lightly floured surface, stretch the pizza dough into a 12- to 14-inch round. Transfer the dough to a piece of parchment paper, then slide the parchment with the dough onto a pizza peel or another inverted baking sheet.

3. Drizzle the dough with olive oil and rub it in; sprinkle with the garlic. Top with the taleggio, brussels sprouts, pancetta and pecorino.

4. Slide the pizza (on the parchment) onto the hot stone and bake until the crust is golden, 10 to 14 minutes. Drizzle with more olive oil and sprinkle with red pepper flakes and salt.

Mini Bacon-and-Egg Pizzas

ACTIVE: 30 min | TOTAL: 45 min (plus 1½ hr rising) | SERVES: 4

FOR THE DOUGH
3¾ cups all-purpose flour, plus more for dusting
1½ teaspoons salt
1⅓ cups warm water (100° to 110°)
1 tablespoon sugar
1 ¼-ounce packet active dry yeast
3 tablespoons extra-virgin olive oil, plus more for brushing

FOR THE PIZZAS
4 slices thick-cut bacon, diced
4 large eggs
Extra-virgin olive oil, for drizzling
Kosher salt and freshly ground pepper
Baby greens, for topping

1. Make the dough: Whisk the flour and salt in a large bowl. Make a well in the middle and add the water, sugar and yeast to the well. Set aside until foamy, then add the olive oil and mix everything together. Knead until the dough is smooth, about 5 minutes. Brush a large bowl generously with olive oil and add the dough, turning to coat. Cover and let rise until doubled in size, about 1½ hours. Meanwhile, place a pizza stone or inverted baking sheet on the lowest oven rack and preheat to 500°.

2. Divide the dough into 2 balls. (You will need only 1 ball of dough for these pizzas; refrigerate or freeze the other ball of dough for another use.) Divide the remaining dough ball into 4 equal pieces. Stretch each piece into a 6-inch round on a floured pizza peel, large wooden cutting board or sheet of parchment paper.

3. Make the pizzas: Sprinkle the bacon evenly onto the dough rounds. Slide onto the hot stone and bake until the bacon is crisp, about 10 minutes.

4. Crack an egg onto each crust and drizzle with olive oil; season with salt and pepper. Bake until the eggs are set, about 5 minutes. Top with baby greens.

Arugula gives this pizza a peppery bite.

Arugula-Prosciutto Pizza

ACTIVE: 25 min **|** TOTAL: 35 min **|** SERVES: 4

1 pound pizza dough, at room temperature (see page 15 or use store-bought)
All-purpose flour, for dusting
Cornmeal, for dusting
¼ cup extra-virgin olive oil
1 clove garlic, grated
½ teaspoon chopped fresh rosemary
Kosher salt and freshly ground pepper
½ cup part-skim ricotta cheese
1 cup shredded mozzarella cheese
4 cups baby arugula
1 small shallot, thinly sliced
Juice of ½ lemon
3 ounces thinly sliced prosciutto
Shaved parmesan cheese, for topping

1. Place a pizza stone or inverted baking sheet in the oven; preheat to 450°. Roll out the dough on a lightly floured surface into a 12-inch round. Transfer to a cornmeal-dusted pizza peel or another inverted baking sheet; slide the dough onto the hot stone. Bake 8 minutes. Meanwhile, combine 2 tablespoons olive oil in a bowl with the garlic, rosemary, and salt and pepper to taste.

2. Remove the crust from the oven, brush with the olive oil mixture and top with the ricotta and mozzarella. Return to the oven; bake until the cheese is golden and bubbly, about 6 more minutes.

3. Meanwhile, toss the arugula and shallot in a large bowl with the lemon juice, the remaining 2 tablespoons olive oil, and salt and pepper to taste. Top the pizza with the arugula salad, prosciutto and shaved parmesan.

PRO TIPS

Cornmeal works well to prevent pizza dough from sticking to a pizza peel. You can also use all-purpose flour or semolina.

Prosciutto can get rubbery in the oven; add it to your pizza after baking.

A vegetable peeler is perfect for shaving hard cheeses like parmesan, pecorino and ricotta salata.

Pizza with Clams and Broccoli Rabe

ACTIVE: 1 hr **I** TOTAL: 1 hr 15 min (plus 1½ hr rising) **I** SERVES: 4

FOR THE DOUGH

1½ teaspoons active dry yeast
1½ cups warm water
 (100˚ to 110˚)
2 cups bread flour
1¾ cups all-purpose flour, plus
 more for kneading
2 teaspoons sugar
2 teaspoons kosher salt
2 tablespoons extra-virgin
 olive oil, plus more for
 the bowl

FOR THE PIZZA

1 pounds littleneck clams
Kosher salt
6 ounces broccoli rabe,
 trimmed
2 tablespoons extra-virgin
 olive oil
1 shallot, thinly sliced
3 cloves garlic, minced
1 cup dry white wine
2 oregano sprigs
⅓ cup heavy cream
All-purpose flour or cornmeal,
 for dusting
⅓ cup grated parmesan
 cheese
1 tablespoon thinly sliced
 jarred Calabrian chiles
Chopped fresh parsley, for
 topping
Lemon wedges, for serving

1. Make the dough: Sprinkle the yeast over the warm water in a small bowl. Let stand until slightly foamy, 5 to 10 minutes. Meanwhile, whisk the bread flour, all-purpose flour, sugar and salt in a large bowl and make a well in the center. Pour the yeast mixture into the well and add the olive oil. Stir with a wooden spoon until a shaggy dough forms. Turn out the dough onto a floured surface, dust the dough with flour and knead, dusting with more flour as needed, until smooth and elastic but still slightly tacky, 3 to 5 minutes.

2. Transfer the dough to an oiled bowl, turning to coat. Cover with plastic wrap and let rise in a warm place until doubled in size, about 1½ hours. Meanwhile, preheat the oven to 500˚ (use the convection setting, if available) with a pizza stone, baking steel or inverted large baking sheet in the lower third of the oven.

3. Toward the end of the rising time, prepare the pizza. Put the clams in a large bowl of cold water; let sit 20 minutes to remove any excess grit. Meanwhile, bring a pot of salted water to a boil. Add the broccoli rabe and cook until bright green and just tender, 2 to 3 minutes. Drain and transfer to a large bowl of ice water. Drain and pat dry, then roughly chop.

4. Drain the clams and rinse under cold water. Heat the olive oil in a large skillet over medium heat. Add the shallot and cook, stirring, until softened, 2 to 3 minutes. Add the garlic and cook until softened, 1 minute. Stir in the wine, oregano and clams. Cover and cook until the clams open, 5 to 7 minutes. Transfer the clams to a bowl with tongs, reserving the cooking liquid in the skillet; discard any unopened clams.

5. Simmer the clam cooking liquid over medium heat until reduced by two-thirds, 10 to 15 minutes. Reduce the heat to low and whisk in the heavy cream. Return the heat to medium, bring to a simmer and cook until thickened and the sauce coats the back of a spoon, 2 to 4 minutes. Let cool until thickened, about 5 minutes; discard the oregano sprigs. Remove the clams from their shells and roughly chop.

6. Divide the dough into 2 balls. (You will need only 1 ball of dough for this pizza; refrigerate or freeze the other ball of dough for another use.) Working on a floured or cornmeal-dusted piece of parchment paper, gently stretch the remaining dough ball into a 12- to 13-inch round. Sprinkle all over with the parmesan, then top with the clam sauce (the sauce will spread as it bakes). Top with the clams, broccoli rabe and Calabrian chiles.

7. Transfer the pizza (on the parchment) to the hot stone and bake until the crust is golden brown, 12 to 15 minutes. Sprinkle with parsley and serve with lemon wedges.

Potatoes just might be your new favorite pizza topping!

Potato and Bacon Pizza

ACTIVE: 30 min **I** TOTAL: 1 hr 5 min **I** SERVES: 4

¼   cup extra-virgin olive oil
1   pound pizza dough,
    at room temperature
    (see page 15 or use
    store-bought)
1½ pounds Yukon Gold
    potatoes (4 medium)
Kosher salt and freshly ground
    pepper
3   slices bacon, diced
3   ounces Cambozola cheese,
    rind removed, cut into
    1-inch pieces
Chopped fresh chives, for
    topping

1. Place a pizza stone or inverted baking sheet in the upper third of the oven and preheat to 475°. Brush a large piece of parchment paper with 2 tablespoons olive oil. Stretch the pizza dough into an 11-by-15-inch rectangle on the parchment. Transfer the dough (on the parchment) to a pizza peel or another inverted baking sheet; set aside.

2. Peel and very thinly slice the potatoes with a mandoline or knife and place in a large microwave-safe bowl. Cover with plastic wrap and microwave until tender, 3 to 4 minutes. Uncover and toss the potatoes with the remaining 2 tablespoons olive oil, 1 teaspoon salt and a few grinds of pepper until fully coated.

3. Spread the potatoes all over the pizza dough, with a slightly thinner layer in the center. Top with the bacon. Slide the pizza (on the parchment) onto the hot stone and bake until the crust is golden and the potatoes are tender and crisp around the edges, 30 to 35 minutes. Remove from the oven and dot with the cheese, then return to the oven and continue baking until the cheese just melts, 1 to 2 minutes. Sprinkle with chives.

PRO TIPS

To make raw bacon easier to dice, lay the strips in a single layer on a plate and freeze until firm, about 20 to 30 minutes.

Cambozola is like a cross between Camembert and gorgonzola. You can also use any kind of blue brie cheese.

Chives are best used raw—heat can dull their delicate flavor. Sprinkle them on your pizza after it comes out of the oven.

Sausage Pizza with Arugula and Grapes

ACTIVE: 30 min **I** TOTAL: 30 min **I** SERVES: 4

4 teaspoons extra-virgin olive oil

1 pound pizza dough, at room temperature (see page 15 or use store-bought)

½ cup ricotta cheese

Kosher salt and freshly ground pepper

2 teaspoons chopped fresh thyme

2 ounces Cambozola cheese, rind removed, cut into ¼-inch pieces

⅔ cup red seedless grapes, halved

2 links hot Italian sausage (about 6 ounces), casings removed, broken into marble-size pieces

½ small shallot, thinly sliced and separated into rings

1 tablespoon honey

1 cup baby arugula

1. Put a pizza stone or inverted baking sheet on the lowest rack of the oven and preheat to 450˚. Place a piece of parchment paper on another inverted baking sheet and brush with 2 teaspoons olive oil. Stretch and lightly pat the pizza dough into a 10-by-14-inch rectangle on the parchment. Prick the dough with a fork everywhere but the edges. Brush with the remaining 2 teaspoons olive oil. Slide the dough (on the parchment) onto the hot stone and bake until lightly browned on the bottom, about 8 minutes.

2. Season the ricotta with ¼ teaspoon salt and a few grinds of pepper. Remove the crust from the oven and spread the ricotta on top. Sprinkle with the thyme and top with the Cambozola, grapes and sausage. Slide back onto the hot stone and continue baking until the sausage is cooked through and the crust is golden, about 10 minutes.

3. Remove from the oven and immediately scatter the shallot rings on top. Drizzle with the honey and top with the arugula.

PRO TIPS

Be sure to break the sausage into small pieces so they cook through in the oven.

Ricotta is rich and creamy, but it can be a bit bland. Season it with salt and pepper to bring out the flavor.

Shallots are milder and slightly sweeter than regular onions. They make for a great raw pizza topping.

Get a little bit of everything with this four-topping pizza!

Quattro Stagioni Pizzas

ACTIVE: 40 min **I** TOTAL: 1 hr (plus 1½ hr rising) **I** SERVES: 4

FOR THE DOUGH

3¾	cups all-purpose flour, plus more for dusting
1½	teaspoons salt
1⅓	cups warm water (100° to 110°)
1	tablespoon sugar
1	¼-ounce packet active dry yeast
3	tablespoons extra-virgin olive oil, plus more for brushing

FOR THE PIZZAS

	Extra-virgin olive oil, for drizzling
4	ounces white mushrooms, thinly sliced
½	cup crushed San Marzano tomatoes
½	teaspoon dried oregano
	Kosher salt and freshly ground pepper
12	oil-cured olives, halved
4	jarred artichoke hearts, quartered lengthwise
2	thin slices Black Forest ham, cut into large pieces
½	pound diced mozzarella cheese

1. Make the dough: Whisk the flour and salt in a large bowl. Make a well in the middle and add the water, sugar and yeast to the well. Set aside until foamy, then add the olive oil and mix everything together. Knead until the dough is smooth, about 5 minutes. Brush a large bowl generously with olive oil and add the dough, turning to coat. Cover and let rise until doubled in size, about 1½ hours. Meanwhile, place a pizza stone or inverted baking sheet on the lowest oven rack and preheat to 500°.

2. Divide the dough into 2 balls. (You will need only 1 ball of dough for these pizzas; refrigerate or freeze the other ball of dough for another use.) Divide the remaining dough ball into 2 pieces. Stretch each piece into a thin 9-inch round on a floured pizza peel, large wooden cutting board or sheet of parchment paper.

3. Make the pizzas: Drizzle a medium skillet with olive oil and heat over medium-high heat. Add the mushrooms and cook, stirring, until wilted and golden, about 5 minutes. Top each dough round with the tomatoes and oregano; season with salt and pepper and drizzle with olive oil. Slide the pizzas onto the hot stone and bake until the crust is golden, about 15 minutes.

4. Top the pizzas with the olives, artichoke hearts, ham and sautéed mushrooms in 4 sections. Sprinkle with the mozzarella. Return the pizzas to the oven and bake until the cheese melts, about 5 minutes. Drizzle with more olive oil.

PRO TIPS

To clean mushrooms, brush off any dirt or wipe clean with a damp cloth. Avoid running under water or the mushrooms will become waterlogged.

Quattro stagioni means "four seasons" in Italian. For a classic look, arrange the toppings in quadrants.

Barbecue Mushroom Pizza

ACTIVE: 30 min | TOTAL: 50 min | SERVES: 6 to 8

¼   cup apple cider vinegar
1   teaspoon sugar
Kosher salt
¼   small red onion, thinly sliced
6   tablespoons extra-virgin olive oil
¾   pound oyster mushrooms, torn into thin strips
Freshly ground pepper
3   cloves garlic, finely chopped
⅓   cup plus ¼ cup barbecue sauce
1   pound pizza dough, at room temperature (see page 15 or use store-bought)
4   ounces smoked gouda cheese, shredded (about 1⅓ cups)
2   ounces monterey jack cheese, shredded (about ½ cup)
1   scallion, thinly sliced
2   tablespoons chopped fresh cilantro

1. Place a pizza stone or inverted baking sheet on the middle oven rack and preheat to 450°. Whisk the vinegar, sugar and a pinch of salt in a small bowl, then add the sliced red onion and submerge in the vinegar; set aside to pickle.

2. Heat 3 tablespoons olive oil in a large nonstick skillet over medium-high heat. Add the mushrooms, season with salt and pepper and cook, undisturbed, until golden brown on the bottom, 5 minutes. Stir and continue to cook, stirring occasionally, until crisp in spots and golden brown, 5 more minutes. Add the garlic and cook, stirring, 1 minute. Add ⅓ cup barbecue sauce and 2 tablespoons water and cook, stirring, until most of the liquid is absorbed and the mushrooms are glazed, 2 to 3 minutes. Remove from the heat.

3. Coat a baking sheet with the remaining 3 tablespoons olive oil. Add the pizza dough and stretch into an 11-by-13-inch oval. Top with the remaining ¼ cup barbecue sauce and spread using the back of a spoon, leaving a ½-inch border. Sprinkle with the gouda, then top with the mushrooms, then the monterey jack. Put the baking sheet directly on the hot stone. Bake until the crust is golden brown on the bottom and around the edge, 15 to 20 minutes.

4. Slide the pizza onto a large cutting board. Drain the red onion and scatter over the pizza, along with the scallion and cilantro.

PRO TIPS

Shredded oyster mushrooms make a great stand-in for pulled meat. Tear the mushrooms into pieces with your fingers.

To shape the crust, stretch the dough on the oiled baking sheet. If it springs back, let it rest about 10 minutes, then try again.

Smoked gouda cheese gives this pie extra meaty flavor without the meat. You can also use smoked cheddar.

Sausage Pizza with Spinach Salad

ACTIVE: 40 min **I** TOTAL: 50 min **I** SERVES: 4

FOR THE PIZZA

1	pound pizza dough, at room temperature (see page 15 or use store-bought)

All-purpose flour, for dusting

1	tablespoon extra-virgin olive oil
½	pound sweet Italian sausage, casings removed
¾	cup whole-milk ricotta cheese
½	cup shredded mozzarella cheese
½	cup shredded provolone cheese
⅓	cup grated parmesan cheese
2	cloves garlic, minced
¼	teaspoon dried oregano

FOR THE SALAD

½	small red onion, thinly sliced
4	cups baby spinach (about 2½ ounces)
1	small bulb fennel, trimmed, cored and thinly sliced
½	cup chopped roasted red peppers
¾	cup quartered marinated artichoke hearts, drained and halved
1	tablespoon red wine vinegar
1	tablespoon extra-virgin olive oil

Kosher salt and freshly ground pepper

Red pepper flakes, for topping

1. Make the pizza: Place a pizza stone or inverted baking sheet on the lowest oven rack; preheat to 475°. Stretch the pizza dough into an 11-by-15-inch rectangle on a floured piece of parchment paper; trim any excess paper around the dough. Transfer the dough (on the parchment) to a pizza peel or another inverted baking sheet and slide the dough and parchment onto the hot stone. Bake until browned in spots, 10 to 12 minutes. Remove the crust from the oven.

2. Meanwhile, heat the olive oil in a medium skillet over medium-high heat. Add the sausage and cook, breaking it up into pieces with a wooden spoon, until no longer pink, about 4 minutes.

3. Spread the ricotta on top of the hot crust, leaving a 1-inch border. Sprinkle with the mozzarella, provolone and parmesan; top with the sausage and garlic. Return the pizza to the oven and bake until the cheese is bubbling, 8 to 10 minutes. Sprinkle with the oregano.

4. Meanwhile, make the salad: Soak the red onion in ice water for 10 minutes, then drain. Toss the spinach, fennel, roasted red peppers, artichoke hearts and red onion in a large bowl with the vinegar and olive oil; season with salt and pepper. Top the pizza with the salad and sprinkle with red pepper flakes.

Everything Bagel Pizza

ACTIVE: 35 min **|** TOTAL: 1 hr **|** SERVES: 4 to 6

3 tablespoons extra-virgin olive oil
1 shallot, finely chopped
3 cloves garlic (2 finely chopped, 1 grated)
Freshly ground pepper
2 tablespoons sesame seeds
1 tablespoon poppy seeds
2 teaspoons coarse sea salt
1½ teaspoons caraway seeds
Coarse cornmeal, for dusting
1 pound pizza dough, at room temperature (see page 15 or use store-bought)
⅓ cup ricotta cheese
¼ cup grated parmesan cheese
¼ teaspoon chopped fresh oregano or rosemary
Pinch of red pepper flakes
Kosher salt
2 ounces fresh mozzarella, thinly sliced

1. Place a pizza stone or inverted baking sheet on the lowest oven rack; preheat to 450˚.

2. Heat 1 tablespoon olive oil in a small skillet over medium heat. Add the shallot and chopped garlic and cook, stirring often, until softened but not browned, 3 to 5 minutes; season with pepper. Transfer to a bowl to cool.

3. Combine the sesame seeds, poppy seeds, coarse salt and caraway seeds in a small bowl. Sprinkle a sheet of parchment paper with cornmeal. Stretch the pizza dough on the parchment into a 12-inch round, pressing with your fingertips. Spread the shallot mixture around the edge of the dough and top with the seed mixture.

4. Combine the ricotta, parmesan, the remaining 2 tablespoons olive oil, the grated garlic, oregano and red pepper flakes in a bowl; season with kosher salt. Spread the ricotta mixture in the middle of the dough. Top with the mozzarella.

5. Slide the parchment onto a pizza peel or another inverted baking sheet, then slide the pizza (on the parchment) onto the hot stone. Bake until the crust is puffed and browned and the cheese is golden in spots, 13 to 15 minutes.

PRO TIPS

You can mix your own everything seasoning as the recipe directs or buy a bottle of premade seasoning.

When stretching pizza dough, lightly oil your hands if the dough is too sticky.

If you want to add veggies, top the pie with cooked broccoli before adding the mozzarella.

Give your crust the everything bagel treatment!

Taco Pizza

ACTIVE: 25 min ▎ TOTAL: 30 min ▎ SERVES: 4 to 6

1   pound pizza dough, at
     room temperature (see
     page 15 or use store-
     bought)
All-purpose flour, for sprinkling
Extra-virgin olive oil, for
     brushing
¾   cup canned refried black
     beans
½   cup salsa
1½   cups grated sharp cheddar
     cheese
3   scallions, finely chopped
¼   cup sliced pickled
     jalapeños
¼   cup sour cream
Juice of 1 lime
Thinly sliced romaine lettuce,
     for topping
Diced tomato, for topping
Kosher salt
¼   cup fresh cilantro

1. Place a pizza stone or inverted baking sheet on the bottom rack of the oven; preheat to 450°. Roll out the pizza dough on a lightly floured work surface into an 11-inch round. Transfer to a parchment-covered pizza peel or another inverted baking sheet.

2. Brush the dough with olive oil, then spread the refried beans on top, leaving a ½-inch border. Spoon the salsa over the beans and sprinkle with the cheese. Scatter the scallions and jalapeños on top. Slide the pizza (on the parchment) onto the hot stone and bake until the crust is crisp, 8 to 10 minutes. Let cool a few minutes.

3. While the pizza is baking, combine the sour cream, half of the lime juice and 1 tablespoon water in a small bowl. In another bowl, toss the lettuce, tomato, and lime juice to taste; season with salt.

4. Top the pizza with the salad, then drizzle with the sour cream mixture and sprinkle with the cilantro.

PRO TIPS

Many pizzerias will sell you a ball of dough— you just have to ask!

To keep this pie vegetarian, check the label on the refried beans—some are made with pork fat.

Add more of your favorite taco toppings to this pizza: Try diced avocado, sliced radishes or crumbled cotija cheese.

White Pizza with Broccolini

ACTIVE: 20 min **I** TOTAL: 40 min **I** SERVES: 4

3 tablespoons extra-virgin olive oil, plus more for drizzling
1 pound pizza dough, at room temperature (see page 15 or use store-bought)
8 ounces ricotta cheese (about 1 cup)
2 cups shredded part-skim mozzarella cheese
½ cup grated parmesan cheese
¼ cup grated pecorino romano cheese
Pinch of red pepper flakes
Kosher salt and freshly ground pepper
8 scallions, greens sliced, whites cut into 1½-inch pieces
¼ cup chopped fresh herbs (such as mint, parsley, dill and/or basil)
2 bunches broccolini, halved lengthwise and roughly chopped

1. Position a rack in the lower third of the oven. Place a pizza stone or inverted baking sheet on the rack and preheat to 500°. Cover another inverted baking sheet with parchment paper and brush with 2 tablespoons olive oil. Put the pizza dough on the oiled parchment and turn to coat. Cover with another piece of parchment and set aside.

2. Mix the 4 cheeses, red pepper flakes and salt and pepper to taste in a bowl. Combine the scallion greens and herbs in another bowl. Toss the broccolini and scallion whites on a baking sheet with the remaining 1 tablespoon olive oil and salt and pepper to taste. Roast 15 minutes.

3. Uncover the dough; stretch into a 12-by-16-inch rectangle. Season with salt and pepper, then slide the dough (on the parchment) onto the hot stone. Bake until golden, 6 to 8 minutes.

4. Slide the crust (on the parchment) back onto the baking sheet and remove from the oven. Top with the cheese mixture, then the roasted vegetables and herb mixture. Return the pizza to the oven and bake until the cheese melts, about 3 more minutes. Drizzle with olive oil.

PRO TIPS

Broccolini is often confused with broccoli rabe, but they're not the same. Broccolini is less bitter.

For extra flavor, season your pizza dough with salt and pepper before adding the toppings.

This is a fun
twist on the usual
St. Patrick's Day
combo!

Corned Beef and Cabbage Pizzas

ACTIVE: 25 min **I** TOTAL: 40 min **I** SERVES: 4

1   pound Yukon Gold potatoes (2 to 4), very thinly sliced
2   tablespoons extra-virgin olive oil
Kosher salt and freshly ground pepper
4   cups very thinly sliced green cabbage (from about ¼ head)
All-purpose flour, for dusting
1   pound pizza dough, cut into 4 pieces, at room temperature (see page 15 or use store-bought)
1   cup shredded white cheddar cheese (about 4 ounces)
1½ cups shredded low-moisture mozzarella cheese (about 6 ounces)
4   ounces cooked corned beef, chopped
Chopped fresh parsley and grated parmesan cheese, for topping

1. Preheat the oven to 475°. Line 2 baking sheets with parchment paper. Toss the sliced potatoes with 1 tablespoon olive oil and a big pinch each of salt and pepper. Spread out on the pans and bake until just tender, 8 to 10 minutes. When cool enough to handle, remove the potatoes to a plate. Put new parchment paper on the baking sheets.

2. Meanwhile, heat the remaining 1 tablespoon olive oil in a large nonstick skillet over medium-high heat. Add the cabbage and a big pinch each of salt and pepper. Cook, stirring occasionally, until tender but not browned, 5 to 7 minutes. Remove from the heat.

3. Lightly dust a work surface with flour. Press each piece of pizza dough into a small round, then use a rolling pin to roll each into an 8-inch round. Put 2 dough rounds on each baking sheet. Scatter the cheddar to the edge of each piece of dough. Top with a layer of potatoes, then top with the mozzarella, cabbage and corned beef.

4. Bake the pizzas until the crust is golden brown and the cheese is melted and bubbly, 10 to 12 minutes. Top with parsley and parmesan.

PRO TIPS

No need to peel the potatoes for this pizza. Yukon Gold potato skins are very thin.

You can use leftover corned beef or buy thick-cut corned beef from the deli counter and chop it up.

Sicilian
Pizza with
Sausage and
Peppers

page 90

Pan PIZZAS

Choose from deep-dish, Sicilian-style, sheet-pan and skillet pizzas. This category has something for everyone!

Sheet-Pan Pizza with Potatoes and Fennel

ACTIVE: 1 hr 20 min **I** TOTAL: 1 hr 40 min (plus 2 hr rising) **I** SERVES: 6

FOR THE DOUGH

- 4 cups bread flour, plus more for dusting
- 2 teaspoons kosher salt
- 1 teaspoon rapid-rise instant yeast
- 2 cups warm water (100° to 110°)
- 5 tablespoons extra-virgin olive oil, plus more for the bowl

FOR THE POTATOES

- 2 russet potatoes (about 1 pound), quartered
- 1 clove garlic
- ½ small bulb fennel, cored and thinly sliced, plus 2 tablespoons chopped fronds

Kosher salt

- ⅓ cup extra-virgin olive oil

Freshly ground pepper

FOR THE PIZZA

- 6 ounces taleggio cheese, rind removed, thinly sliced
- ½ small fennel bulb, cored and thinly sliced
- ½ cup grated parmesan cheese
- 1 tablespoon extra-virgin olive oil

Kosher salt and freshly ground pepper

1. Make the dough: Combine the flour, salt and yeast in a large bowl. Stir in the water and 2 tablespoons olive oil with a wooden spoon until a shaggy dough forms. Cover with plastic wrap and let rise in a warm place until the dough rises slightly, about 1 hour.

2. Using lightly floured hands, transfer the dough to a generously floured surface and knead several times until it just starts to become smooth and elastic, about 1 minute (do not over-knead). Transfer to a lightly oiled large bowl. Tightly cover with plastic wrap and let rise in a warm place until almost doubled in size, about 1 hour. Meanwhile, place a pizza stone or inverted rimmed baking sheet on the lower oven rack and preheat to 500°.

3. Divide the dough into 2 balls. (You will need only 1 ball of dough for this pizza; refrigerate or freeze the other ball of dough for another use.) Brush a 13-by-18-inch rimmed baking sheet (not nonstick) with the remaining 3 tablespoons olive oil. Place the remaining dough ball on the baking sheet and cover with plastic wrap, then press firmly with your hands to fill the baking sheet. (If the dough is hard to stretch, keep it covered and let rest up to 30 more minutes.)

4. Remove the plastic wrap and transfer the baking sheet to the hot pizza stone. Bake until the crust starts browning, about 10 minutes. Remove from the oven and carefully loosen the crust from the pan using a spatula. Leave the oven on.

5. Meanwhile, make the potatoes: Combine the potatoes, garlic, sliced fennel and fennel fronds in a large pot of salted water. Bring to a boil, then reduce the heat to medium; cook until the potatoes are very tender, about 15 minutes. Drain and return to the pot. Add the olive oil and mash until almost smooth. Stir in 1 teaspoon salt and a few grinds of pepper; set aside.

6. Assemble the pizza: Keep the prebaked crust on the baking sheet. Scatter the taleggio and the potato mixture over the crust, spreading the potato mixture slightly. Scatter the sliced fennel on top, sprinkle with the parmesan and drizzle with the olive oil. Transfer the baking sheet to the hot pizza stone and bake until the cheese melts and the crust is golden brown, 10 to 12 minutes. Remove from the oven and season with salt and pepper.

PRO TIP

You can bake the crust up to 8 hours ahead. Follow the recipe through step 4; let the crust cool, then wrap in plastic wrap. Finish making the pizza when you're ready to eat.

Sicilian pizza is made with a focaccia-like dough.

Basic Sicilian Pizza

ACTIVE: 40 min **I** TOTAL: 1 hr 20 min (plus overnight and 2 hr rising) **I** SERVES: 8

FOR THE DOUGH
- 4 cups all-purpose flour, plus more for dusting
- 2 teaspoons sugar
- 2 teaspoons kosher salt
- 1 teaspoon instant yeast
- 1¾ cups warm water (100˚ to 110˚)
- 6 tablespoons extra-virgin olive oil, plus more for the bowl

FOR THE PIZZA
- 1 28-ounce can whole peeled tomatoes (preferably San Marzano)
- 1½ teaspoons kosher salt, plus more for sprinkling
- 12 ounces whole milk mozzarella cheese, thinly sliced

1. Make the dough: Whisk the flour, sugar, salt and yeast in a medium bowl. Pour the warm water into a large bowl, then add the flour mixture and stir until combined. Stir in 2 tablespoons olive oil to make a very sticky dough. Turn out onto a lightly floured surface and knead, dusting with more flour as needed, until the dough comes together and no longer sticks to your fingers, about 2 minutes. Transfer to a lightly oiled large bowl and turn to coat. Tightly cover with plastic wrap and refrigerate overnight.

2. Coat an 11-by-17-inch rimmed baking sheet with 3 tablespoons olive oil. Add the dough and stretch it to fit the baking sheet. Brush with the remaining 1 tablespoon olive oil. Loosely cover with plastic wrap and let rise at room temperature until puffy, about 2 hours.

3. Make the pizza: Position a rack in the upper third of the oven and preheat to 450˚. Combine the tomatoes and their juices and the salt in a medium bowl and crush well with your hands or a potato masher. Uncover the dough and sprinkle with salt. Gently place the baking sheet in the oven and bake until the crust is golden, about 20 minutes. Remove the crust from the oven, top with the sliced mozzarella and cover with 2 cups of the crushed tomatoes. Bake until the cheese is bubbling through the sauce and starts browning, 15 to 20 more minutes.

4. Let the pizza stand 10 minutes, then remove from the pan using a spatula and transfer to a cutting board. Let cool 1 to 2 minutes before slicing.

PRO TIPS

When putting the crust in the oven, be gentle: If you knock the baking sheet, the dough could deflate—and you want it to stay puffy.

Good-quality canned tomatoes make a big difference in this pizza. Look for San Marzano tomatoes from Italy.

Sicilian Pizza with Sausage and Peppers

ACTIVE: 30 min | TOTAL: 1 hr | SERVES: 6

1   tablespoon extra-virgin olive oil

2   1-pound balls pizza dough, at room temperature (see page 15 or use store-bought)

⅔   cup canned crushed tomatoes

¼   teaspoon red pepper flakes

1½   cups shredded mozzarella cheese or Italian cheese blend

½   pound sweet Italian sausage, casings removed, crumbled

1   green bell pepper, sliced into rings

1. Preheat the oven to 450°. Drizzle the olive oil into a 10-by-15-inch baking dish or onto a rimmed baking sheet. Place the balls of dough side by side in the baking dish and pinch the edges together to make 1 large piece of dough. Press and stretch the dough so it fills the dish. (If using a baking sheet, press and stretch the dough into a 10-by-15-inch rectangle.)

2. Spread the crushed tomatoes over the dough, leaving a 1-inch border around the edges. Top with the red pepper flakes, cheese, sausage and bell pepper.

3. Bake the pizza until the crust is golden brown and the sausage is fully cooked, 25 to 30 minutes. Let cool slightly before slicing.

PRO TIPS

If you use refrigerated dough, bring it to room temperature at least 30 minutes before you start.

To add some spice to this pizza, use hot Italian sausage and sprinkle with extra red pepper flakes before serving.

Let pizza cool slightly before you slice it. The cheese and toppings need to rest for a bit to set up.

You can make this pizza in a baking dish or on a sheet pan.

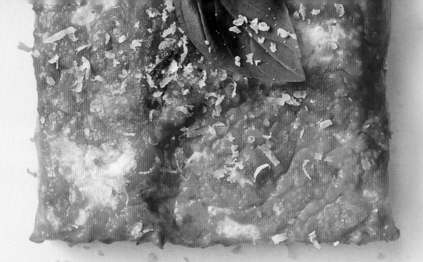

This pie is made in reverse— there's a layer of cheese under the sauce.

Sheet-Pan Pizza alla Vodka

ACTIVE: 1 hr 15 min **I** TOTAL: 1 hr 35 min (plus 2 hr 45 min rising) **I** SERVES: 6 to 8

FOR THE DOUGH
4   cups all-purpose flour
1   tablespoon sugar
2   teaspoons kosher salt
1¼ teaspoons active dry yeast
1½ cups warm water
    (100° to 110°)
⅓   cup plus 2 tablespoons
    extra-virgin olive oil

FOR THE SAUCE
3   tablespoons extra-virgin
    olive oil
1   small onion, chopped
3   cloves garlic, minced
Pinch of red pepper flakes
2   tablespoons tomato paste
1   28-ounce can whole
    peeled tomatoes
Kosher salt
1   cup heavy cream
¼   cup vodka

FOR THE PIZZA
¼   cup grated pecorino
    romano cheese, plus more
    for topping
¼   cup grated parmesan
    cheese, plus more
    for topping
1   pound fresh mozzarella
    cheese, sliced
Fresh basil, for topping

1. Make the dough: Combine the flour, sugar, salt and yeast in a stand mixer fitted with the dough hook. Combine the warm water and 2 tablespoons olive oil, then add to the mixer on low speed and mix until a loose ball forms. Knead the dough with the mixer on medium-high speed until smooth and slightly tacky, about 7 minutes.

2. Pour the remaining ⅓ cup olive oil into an 11-by-17-inch rimmed baking sheet or black steel pan. Transfer the ball of dough to the pan, turning to coat with the oil. Cover loosely with plastic wrap and let rise in a warm place until the dough fills about two-thirds of the pan, 1½ to 2 hours.

3. Slide your hands under the dough and lift, gently stretching the dough to fit the pan. (It's OK if it doesn't stretch to the corners.) For the final rise, cover the dough with plastic wrap and set aside until slightly puffy, 30 to 45 minutes. Meanwhile, put a pizza stone or inverted baking sheet in the lower third of the oven and preheat to 500° for 1 hour.

4. Meanwhile, make the vodka sauce: Heat the olive oil in a medium saucepan over medium-high heat. Add the onion and cook, stirring, until softened, 5 minutes. Add the garlic and red pepper flakes and cook, stirring, until softened, 30 seconds. Add the tomato paste and cook, stirring, 1 minute. Add the tomatoes and ½ teaspoon salt. Bring to a boil, then reduce the heat to a simmer and cook, stirring, until thickened, 12 to 18 minutes. Stir in the heavy cream and simmer until slightly thickened, 3 to 5 minutes. Carefully add the vodka; cook 1 minute. Season with salt. Puree the sauce in a blender. Remove 1 cup sauce to a bowl; set aside for serving. Refrigerate the remaining sauce until cooled.

5. Assemble the pizza: Sprinkle the pecorino and parmesan over the dough. Top with the mozzarella, leaving a ½-inch border. Spoon the cooled vodka sauce over the top. Sprinkle with more grated cheese. Put the baking sheet directly on the hot stone and bake until the crust is browned around the edges and the cheese is bubbling, 15 to 20 minutes. Let cool slightly.

6. Loosen the edges of the pizza with an offset spatula, then loosen the bottom. Slide the pizza onto a cutting board. Top with basil and more grated cheese. Serve with the reserved sauce.

Sheet-Pan Pizza with Arugula Pesto

ACTIVE: 45 min **I** TOTAL: 55 min (plus 2 hr rising) **I** SERVES: 6

FOR THE DOUGH

4	cups bread flour, plus more for dusting
2	teaspoons kosher salt
1	teaspoon rapid-rise instant yeast
2	cups warm water (100° to 110°)
5	tablespoons extra-virgin olive oil, plus more for the bowl

FOR THE PESTO

¼	cup hazelnuts
3	cups baby arugula
1	cup fresh parsley
1	clove garlic
1	tablespoon capers, drained
½	cup extra-virgin olive oil
½	cup grated parmesan cheese

Kosher salt and freshly ground pepper

FOR THE PIZZA

6	ounces fresh mozzarella cheese (preferably buffalo mozzarella), drained and sliced
1	zucchini, very thinly sliced
2	tablespoons grated parmesan cheese
1	tablespoon extra-virgin olive oil

Torn fresh basil, for topping
Kosher salt and freshly ground pepper

1. Make the dough: Combine the flour, salt and yeast in a large bowl. Stir in the water and 2 tablespoons olive oil with a wooden spoon until a shaggy dough forms. Cover with plastic wrap and let rise in a warm place until the dough rises slightly, about 1 hour.

2. Using lightly floured hands, transfer the dough to a generously floured surface and knead several times until it just starts to become smooth and elastic, about 1 minute (do not over-knead). Transfer to a lightly oiled large bowl. Tightly cover with plastic wrap and let rise in a warm place until the dough is almost doubled in size, about 1 hour. Meanwhile, place a pizza stone or inverted rimmed baking sheet on the lower oven rack and preheat to 500°.

3. Divide the dough into 2 balls. (You will need only 1 ball of dough for this pizza; refrigerate or freeze the other ball of dough for another use.) Brush a 13-by-18-inch rimmed baking sheet (not nonstick) with the remaining 3 tablespoons olive oil. Place the remaining dough ball on the baking sheet and cover with plastic wrap, then press firmly with your hands to fill the baking sheet. (If the dough is hard to stretch, keep it covered and let rest up to 30 more minutes.)

4. Remove the plastic wrap and transfer the baking sheet to the hot pizza stone. Bake until the crust starts browning, about 10 minutes. Remove from the oven and carefully loosen the crust from the pan using a spatula. Leave the oven on.

5. Make the pesto: Lightly toast the hazelnuts in a dry skillet over medium-high heat, stirring occasionally, about 5 minutes; let cool. Transfer to a food processor and add the arugula, parsley, garlic and capers; pulse until almost smooth. With the motor running, gradually add the olive oil and process until combined. Add the parmesan and pulse to combine; add 2 tablespoons water to loosen. Season with salt and pepper.

6. Assemble the pizza: Keep the prebaked crust on the baking sheet. Spread with the pesto and top with the mozzarella. Arrange the zucchini in overlapping rows on top. Sprinkle with the parmesan and drizzle with the olive oil. Transfer the baking sheet to the hot pizza stone and bake until the cheese is melted and the crust is golden brown, 10 to 12 minutes. Remove from the oven and top with torn basil; season with salt and pepper.

This pesto is made with arugula and hazelnuts!

Cast iron gets super hot and makes this crust nice and crisp.

Skillet Taco Pizza

ACTIVE: 45 min **I** TOTAL: 1 hr **I** SERVES: 6 to 8

---

1   pound pizza dough, at room temperature (see page 15 or use store-bought)

All-purpose flour, for dusting

3   tablespoons extra-virgin olive oil

2   cloves garlic, sliced

1   15-ounce can crushed fire-roasted tomatoes

½   teaspoon dried oregano

Kosher salt and freshly ground pepper

8   ounces ground beef

1   tablespoon chili powder

1   teaspoon ground cumin

½   teaspoon garlic powder

1   cup shredded cheddar cheese (about 4 ounces)

½   small red onion, thinly sliced

1   cup shredded mozzarella cheese (about 4 ounces)

Shredded lettuce, chopped avocado and pico de gallo, for topping

1. Preheat the oven to 525° (or the highest temperature available). Press and stretch the pizza dough into a 12- to 13-inch circle on a lightly floured surface. Lightly dust the top with flour and cover with a clean kitchen towel.

2. Heat 2 tablespoons olive oil in a medium saucepan over medium-high heat. Add the garlic and cook, stirring occasionally, until lightly browned, about 2 minutes. Add the crushed tomatoes and oregano. Bring to a boil, then reduce the heat to a simmer and cook until thickened and reduced to about 1 cup, 10 to 12 minutes. Season with salt and pepper.

3. Meanwhile, heat a medium skillet over medium-high heat and add the remaining 1 tablespoon olive oil. Add the beef and season with a large pinch of salt and a few grinds of pepper. Cook, breaking up the beef with a wooden spoon, until no longer pink, 4 to 5 minutes. Add the chili powder, cumin and garlic powder and cook, stirring, until combined, 1 to 2 minutes. Transfer the beef mixture to a small bowl with a slotted spoon.

4. Heat a 12-inch cast-iron skillet over medium-high heat. Lightly sprinkle the skillet with flour and immediately add the pizza dough, stretching it as needed to completely cover the bottom of the skillet. Cook until the dough starts to puff slightly, about 2 minutes. Spoon the tomato sauce mixture all over the dough and then spoon the beef mixture on top. Sprinkle with the cheddar, top with the red onion, then sprinkle with the mozzarella. Transfer the skillet to the oven and bake until the cheese is melted and bubbling and the crust is browned around the edge, 10 to 12 minutes. Let cool slightly.

5. Run a small spatula around the edge of the pizza to loosen. Top with lettuce, avocado and pico de gallo.

Deep-Dish Pizza with Spicy Sausage and Olives

ACTIVE: 50 min **I** TOTAL: 1 hr (plus 2½ hr rising) **I** SERVES: 6

FOR THE DOUGH

1½	teaspoons active dry yeast
1½	cups warm water (100˚ to 110˚)
2	cups bread flour
1¾	cups all-purpose flour, plus more for dusting
2	teaspoons sugar
2	teaspoons kosher salt
¼	cup extra-virgin olive oil, plus more for the bowl

FOR THE PIZZA

1	teaspoon extra-virgin olive oil
8	ounces hot Italian sausage (about 3 links), casings removed, pinched into ¾-inch pieces
2	tablespoons grated parmesan cheese, plus more for topping
8	ounces low-moisture mozzarella cheese (half cut into thin slices and half shredded)
½	cup pizza sauce
¼	cup canned sliced black olives, drained

Finely chopped fresh parsley, for topping

1. Make the dough: Sprinkle the yeast over the warm water in a small bowl. Let stand until dissolved and slightly foamy, 5 to 10 minutes. Meanwhile, whisk the bread flour, all-purpose flour, sugar and salt in a large bowl and make a well in the center. Pour the yeast mixture into the well and add 2 tablespoons olive oil. Stir with a wooden spoon until a shaggy dough forms.

2. Turn the dough out onto a lightly floured surface, dust the dough with flour and knead, dusting with more flour as needed, until it's very smooth and elastic but still slightly tacky, 3 to 5 minutes.

3. Transfer the dough to an oiled bowl, turning to coat. Cover with plastic wrap and let rise in a warm place until doubled in size, about 1½ hours.

4. Divide the dough into 2 balls. (You will need only 1 ball of dough for this pizza; refrigerate or freeze the other ball of dough for another use.) Transfer the remaining dough ball to a 9-inch round cake pan coated with the remaining 2 tablespoons olive oil. Cover and let the dough rise again until almost spread to the edge of the pan, about 1 hour.

5. Put a pizza stone, baking steel or inverted large baking sheet in the lower third of the oven. Preheat to 500˚ (use the convection setting, if available).

6. Make the pizza: Heat the olive oil in a medium skillet over medium-high heat. Add the sausage and cook, stirring occasionally, until browned and cooked through, 5 to 7 minutes. Remove to a paper towel–lined plate with a slotted spoon. Let drain and cool.

7. Press the dough to reach the edge of the pan, then press the dough up the side to create a lip that's ½ to ¾ inch higher than the center of the dough. Top with the parmesan and sliced mozzarella, leaving a ½-inch border around the edge. Spread the pizza sauce over the cheese, almost to the edge, and top with the sausage, olives and shredded mozzarella.

8. Place the pan on the hot stone and bake the pizza until the crust is golden brown and the cheese is bubbling and browned in spots, 12 to 15 minutes. Let cool 5 minutes, then loosen the edge with a small offset spatula and remove the pizza to a cutting board. Sprinkle with parmesan and chopped parsley.

PRO TIPS

Put a layer of cheese under the sauce: It prevents the crust from getting soggy and keeps the cheese from over-browning.

If you have a convection setting on your oven, now is a good time to use it. It'll help the thick crust cook more evenly.

PRO TIPS

Don't skip the cornmeal in the dough. It adds a slightly sweet flavor and helps the crust crisp up nicely.

It's OK if the pizza is still jiggly when it comes out of the oven—it will set up as it cools.

This recipe makes two pizzas. To freeze one, let it cool, then wrap in plastic wrap and foil. To reheat it, unwrap and bake at 325° for 50 to 60 minutes.

Basic Deep-Dish Pizzas

ACTIVE: 45 min **I** TOTAL: 1½ hr (plus 1 hr 15 min rising) **I** SERVES: 10

FOR THE DOUGH

4   cups unbleached all-purpose flour
3   tablespoons fine yellow cornmeal
2   teaspoons kosher salt
2½ teaspoons instant yeast
2   tablespoons extra-virgin olive oil, plus more for the bowl
4   tablespoons unsalted butter, melted
2   tablespoons vegetable oil
1   cup plus 2 tablespoons warm water (100˚ to 110˚)

FOR THE PIZZAS

3   tablespoons extra-virgin olive oil, plus more for the pans
2   cloves garlic, grated
½   teaspoon red pepper flakes
1   28-ounce can tomato puree (preferably San Marzano)
1   teaspoon dried oregano
Kosher salt
3   8-ounce packages low-moisture whole-milk mozzarella cheese, thinly sliced

1. Make the dough: Combine the flour, cornmeal, salt, yeast, olive oil, melted butter, vegetable oil and warm water in the bowl of a stand mixer fitted with the dough hook. Mix on medium speed until the dough comes together and pulls away from the side of the bowl but still sticks to the bottom, about 3 minutes. Reduce the mixer speed to low and knead 5 minutes. Transfer the dough to a lightly oiled bowl and turn to coat. Tightly cover with plastic wrap and let rise in a warm place, 1 hour.

2. Meanwhile, make the pizzas: Heat the olive oil in a medium saucepan over medium heat. Add the garlic and red pepper flakes and cook, stirring, until the garlic is slightly softened, about 1 minute. Add the tomato puree and 1 cup water. Stir in the oregano and 1 teaspoon salt. Bring to a boil, then reduce the heat and simmer, stirring occasionally, until slightly thickened, about 8 minutes.

3. Preheat the oven to 425˚. Generously brush two 9½-inch round deep-dish pizza pans (or 9-inch cake pans) with about 3 tablespoons olive oil each. Divide the dough in half; press each half into the bottom of a pan. Let the dough rest, 15 minutes. Push the dough down and press it up the sides of the pans with your fingers. Layer the cheese on top of each crust and spread each with 1½ cups sauce.

4. Bake the pizzas until the crust is dark golden brown and the cheese is bubbling, 40 to 45 minutes (it will still be jiggly in the center). Let cool 15 minutes, then transfer to a cutting board.

Deep-Dish Pepperoni Pizza with Pepperoncini

ACTIVE: 30 min **I** TOTAL: 45 min **I** SERVES: 4 to 6

¼ cup extra-virgin olive oil
1 pound pizza dough, at room
  temperature (see page 15
  or use store-bought)
1½ cups tomato sauce
1 clove garlic, grated
¼ teaspoon dried oregano
Kosher salt and freshly ground
  pepper
¼ onion, thinly sliced
1½ cups shredded mozzarella
  cheese (about 6 ounces)
½ cup chopped pepperoncini,
  plus 2 tablespoons brine
  from the jar
½ cup sliced pepperoni
  (about 3 ounces)
8 fresh basil leaves, thinly
  sliced
1 5-ounce package mixed
  salad greens (about 6 cups)

1. Put a pizza stone or inverted baking sheet on the bottom oven rack; preheat to 475°. Brush the bottom and side of a 10-inch deep-dish pizza pan or a 9-inch round cake pan with 2 tablespoons olive oil. Press the dough into the pan.

2. Combine the tomato sauce, garlic, oregano, ½ teaspoon salt and a few grinds of pepper in a bowl. Spread 1 cup of the sauce over the dough; scatter the onion on top. Transfer the pan to the hot stone; bake until the crust puffs up slightly and starts browning, about 10 minutes.

3. Remove the pizza from the oven; top with the cheese, pepperoncini and pepperoni, then top with the remaining sauce. Return to the hot stone and bake until golden and crisp around the edge, about 12 minutes. Let cool 5 minutes. Top with the basil before slicing.

4. Toss the greens with the remaining 2 tablespoons olive oil and the pepperoncini brine; season with salt and pepper. Serve with the pizza.

PRO TIPS

Use a dark metal pan if you have one; it absorbs heat better than light metal, which means your crust will crisp up better.

Be sure to generously oil the pan, including the inside walls. The crust will puff up a lot in the oven.

To chiffonade basil for garnish, stack the leaves, then roll them up together and thinly slice.

Top the pizza with pepperoncini, then use the brine to dress the salad.

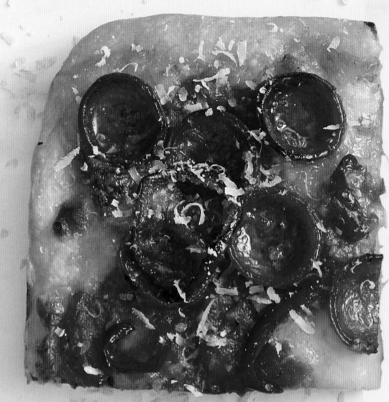

Pepperoni and hot honey are a perfect match!

Sheet-Pan Pepperoni Pizza with Hot Honey

ACTIVE: 45 min | TOTAL: 1 hr (plus 2 hr 45 min rising) | SERVES: 6 to 8

FOR THE DOUGH
4   cups all-purpose flour
1   tablespoon sugar
2   teaspoons kosher salt
1¼   teaspoons active dry yeast
1½   cups warm water
       (100° to 110°)
⅓   cup plus 2 tablespoons
       extra-virgin olive oil

FOR THE SAUCE
1   28-ounce can whole peeled
       tomatoes, drained
2   tablespoons extra-virgin
       olive oil
3   cloves garlic, minced
1   teaspoon dried oregano
½   teaspoon hot honey, plus
       more for drizzling
Kosher salt and freshly ground
       pepper

FOR THE PIZZA
¼   cup grated parmesan
       cheese
12   ounces whole-milk
       mozzarella cheese,
       shredded (about 3 cups)
1½   6-ounce logs pepperoni in
       natural casings, sliced
       ⅛ inch thick
½   cup sliced hot pickled
       cherry peppers, drained

1. Make the dough: Combine the flour, sugar, salt and yeast in a stand mixer fitted with the dough hook. Combine the water and 2 tablespoons olive oil, then add to the mixer on low speed and mix until a loose ball forms. Knead the dough with the mixer on medium-high speed until smooth and slightly tacky, about 7 minutes.

2. Pour the remaining ⅓ cup olive oil into an 11-by-17-inch rimmed baking sheet or black steel pan. Transfer the ball of dough to the pan, turning to coat with the oil. Cover loosely with plastic wrap and let rise in a warm place until the dough fills about two-thirds of the pan, 1½ to 2 hours.

3. Slide your hands under the dough and lift, gently stretching the dough to fit the pan. (It's OK if it doesn't stretch to the corners.) For the final rise, cover the dough with plastic wrap and set aside until slightly puffy, 30 to 45 minutes. Meanwhile, put a pizza stone or inverted baking sheet in the lower third of the oven and preheat to 500° for 1 hour.

4. Meanwhile, make the sauce: Put the tomatoes in a medium saucepan and break them up with your hands or a wooden spoon. Add the olive oil, garlic, oregano, hot honey, ½ teaspoon salt and a few grinds of pepper. Bring to a simmer, stirring often and crushing the tomatoes with a wooden spoon. Continue to simmer, crushing the tomatoes, until the sauce thickens slightly, about 5 minutes. Let cool.

5. Assemble the pizza: Sprinkle 2 tablespoons parmesan over the dough. Sprinkle the mozzarella on top, leaving a ½-inch border. Spoon the tomato sauce over the cheese. Top with the pepperoni and cherry peppers. Put the baking sheet directly on the hot stone and bake until the crust is browned around the edges and the pepperoni is crisp, 15 to 20 minutes. Sprinkle the remaining 2 tablespoons parmesan over the pizza. Let cool slightly.

6. Loosen the edges of the pizza with an offset spatula, then loosen the bottom. Slide the pizza onto a cutting board. Drizzle with hot honey.

Sheet-Pan Hawaiian Pizza

ACTIVE: 40 min I TOTAL: 1 hr (plus 2½ hr rising) I SERVES: 6

FOR THE DOUGH

1½ teaspoons active dry yeast
1½ cups warm water (100° to 110°)
2   cups bread flour
1¾ cups all-purpose flour, plus more for dusting
2   teaspoons sugar
2   teaspoons kosher salt
5   tablespoons extra-virgin olive oil

FOR THE PIZZA

1   cup pizza sauce
1   8-ounce bag shredded part-skim mozzarella cheese (about 2 cups)
6   ounces Canadian bacon, diced
1   20-ounce can sliced pineapple rings, drained and diced
½   green bell pepper, diced
½   red onion, diced
Red pepper flakes, for topping

1. Make the dough: Sprinkle the yeast over the warm water in a small bowl. Let stand until dissolved and slightly foamy, 5 to 10 minutes. Meanwhile, whisk the bread flour, all-purpose flour, sugar and salt in a large bowl and make a well in the center. Pour the yeast mixture into the well and add 2 tablespoons olive oil. Stir with a wooden spoon until a shaggy dough forms.

2. Turn the dough out onto a lightly floured surface, dust the dough with flour and knead, dusting with more flour as needed, until it's very smooth and elastic but still slightly tacky, 3 to 5 minutes.

3. Brush an 11-by-17-inch rimmed baking sheet with the remaining 3 tablespoons olive oil. Add the dough, turning to coat. Cover with plastic wrap and let rise in a warm place until doubled in size, about 2 hours.

4. Put a pizza stone, baking steel or inverted large baking sheet in the lower third of the oven. Preheat to 500° (use the convection setting, if available).

5. Gently stretch and press the dough to cover the pan as much as possible. Let stand 30 minutes, then gently press and stretch the dough again, if needed, to cover the pan.

6. Make the pizza: Top the dough with the pizza sauce, half of the mozzarella, the Canadian bacon, pineapple, bell pepper and red onion, then sprinkle with the remaining mozzarella. Place the baking sheet on the hot stone and bake the pizza until the crust is golden brown, 20 to 24 minutes. Let cool slightly, then remove to a cutting board. Top with red pepper flakes.

PRO TIPS

This recipe makes two pounds of dough. If you use store-bought dough, you'll likely need two packages.

When kneading the dough, dust with flour to prevent sticking, but don't go overboard—too much flour will make your dough dry.

Be sure to use Canadian bacon for this pizza, not regular bacon. Canadian bacon is sold fully cooked; it's more like ham.

Try using buffalo mozzarella on your pizza—it's extra creamy.

108

Sheet-Pan Pizza with Roasted Red Peppers

ACTIVE: 1 hr 20 min ▪ TOTAL: 1 hr 40 min (plus 2 hr rising) ▪ SERVES: 6

FOR THE DOUGH
4   cups bread flour, plus more
     for dusting
2   teaspoons kosher salt
1   teaspoon rapid-rise instant
     yeast
2   cups warm water
     (100° to 110°)
5   tablespoons extra-virgin
     olive oil, plus more for
     the bowl

FOR THE PEPPER SPREAD
1   Fresno or red jalapeño
     chile pepper
1   large red bell pepper
1   clove garlic
2   anchovy fillets
¼   teaspoon red pepper flakes
¼   teaspoon dried oregano
⅓   cup extra-virgin olive oil
Kosher salt

FOR THE PIZZA
¾ to 1 cup tomato sauce
6   ounces fresh mozzarella
     cheese, drained and
     sliced
¼   cup grated parmesan
     cheese
Torn fresh oregano or basil,
     for topping
Kosher salt

1. Make the dough: Combine the flour, salt and yeast in a large bowl. Stir in the water and 2 tablespoons olive oil with a wooden spoon until a shaggy dough forms. Cover with plastic wrap and let rise in a warm place until the dough rises slightly, about 1 hour.

2. Using lightly floured hands, transfer the dough to a generously floured surface and knead several times until it just starts to become smooth and elastic, about 1 minute (do not over-knead). Transfer to a lightly oiled large bowl. Tightly cover with plastic wrap and let rise in a warm place until almost doubled in size, about 1 hour. Meanwhile, place a pizza stone or inverted rimmed baking sheet on the lower oven rack and preheat to 500°.

3. Divide the dough into 2 balls. (You will need only 1 ball of dough for this pizza; refrigerate or freeze the other ball of dough for another use.) Brush a 13-by-18-inch rimmed baking sheet (not nonstick) with the remaining 3 tablespoons olive oil. Place the remaining dough ball on the baking sheet and cover with plastic wrap, then press firmly with your hands to fill the baking sheet. (If the dough is hard to stretch, keep it covered and let rest up to 30 more minutes.)

4. Remove the plastic wrap and transfer the baking sheet to the hot pizza stone. Bake until the crust starts browning, about 10 minutes. Remove from the oven and carefully loosen the crust from the pan using a spatula. Leave the oven on.

5. Make the pepper spread: Roast the chile pepper and bell pepper over the flame of a gas burner (or under the broiler), turning, until charred, 4 minutes for the chile and 6 to 8 minutes for the bell pepper. Transfer the peppers to a bowl, cover with plastic wrap and let cool slightly, about 10 minutes. Peel off the charred skins with your fingers (you may want to use gloves for the chile pepper to avoid irritation). Halve the peppers and remove the seeds. Combine the garlic, anchovies, red pepper flakes and oregano in a food processor. Add the roasted peppers and pulse until almost smooth. Pour in the olive oil and pulse a few times. Season with salt.

6. Assemble the pizza: Keep the prebaked crust on the baking sheet. Spread with the tomato sauce. Top with the mozzarella, then spoon ½ cup pepper spread on top. Sprinkle with half of the parmesan. Transfer the baking sheet to the hot pizza stone and bake until the cheese melts and the crust is golden brown, 10 to 12 minutes. Remove from the oven and top with the remaining parmesan and the herbs. Season with salt.

Sheet-Pan Spinach Pizza with Sesame Seeds

ACTIVE: 1 hr **I** TOTAL: 1 hr 20 min (plus 2 hr 45 min rising) **I** SERVES: 6 to 8

FOR THE DOUGH

- 4 cups all-purpose flour
- 1 tablespoon sugar
- 2 teaspoons kosher salt
- 1¼ teaspoons active dry yeast
- 1½ cups warm water (100° to 110°)
- ⅓ cup plus 2 tablespoons extra-virgin olive oil
- 2 tablespoons sesame seeds

FOR THE PIZZA

- ¼ cup extra-virgin olive oil
- 10 cups loosely packed trimmed spinach leaves (about 10 ounces)
- 3 large cloves garlic, minced

Kosher salt and freshly ground pepper

- 1 cup whole-milk ricotta cheese
- 3 tablespoons grated pecorino romano cheese
- 1 teaspoon chopped fresh oregano
- 1 tablespoon sesame seeds
- 12 ounces whole-milk mozzarella cheese, shredded (about 3 cups)

1. Make the dough: Combine the flour, sugar, salt and yeast in a stand mixer fitted with the dough hook. Combine the water and 2 tablespoons olive oil, then add to the mixer on low speed and mix until a loose ball forms. Knead the dough with the mixer on medium-high speed until smooth and slightly tacky, about 7 minutes.

2. Pour the remaining ⅓ cup olive oil into an 11-by-17-inch rimmed baking sheet or black steel pan. Transfer the ball of dough to the pan, turning to coat with the oil. Shape the dough into an oval and sprinkle with sesame seeds, patting to adhere. Flip the dough, cover loosely with plastic wrap and let rise in a warm place until the dough fills about two-thirds of the pan, 1½ to 2 hours.

3. Slide your hands under the dough and lift, gently stretching the dough to fit the pan. (It's OK if it doesn't stretch to the corners.) For the final rise, cover the dough with plastic wrap and set aside until slightly puffy, 30 to 45 minutes. Meanwhile, put a pizza stone or inverted baking sheet in the lower third of the oven and preheat to 500° for 1 hour.

4. Make the pizza: Heat 2 tablespoons olive oil in a large nonstick skillet over medium-high heat. Add the spinach and cook, tossing with tongs, until wilted, 3 to 4 minutes. Stir in the remaining 2 tablespoons olive oil, the garlic, ½ teaspoon salt and a few grinds of pepper and cook, stirring occasionally, until the water evaporates and the garlic is just golden, about 3 minutes. Remove the spinach to a cutting board and chop. Combine the ricotta, pecorino, oregano and a few grinds of pepper in a small bowl.

5. Sprinkle the sesame seeds around the edge of the dough to create a ¼-inch border, pressing to adhere. Sprinkle the mozzarella over the dough up to the sesame border. Top with the spinach, then top with spoonfuls (about 2 tablespoons each) of the ricotta mixture. Put the baking sheet directly on the hot stone and bake until the crust is browned around the edges and the cheese is golden, 15 to 20 minutes. Let cool slightly.

6. Loosen the edges of the pizza with an offset spatula, then loosen the bottom. Slide the pizza onto a cutting board.

Sesame seeds add flavor and crunch to this crust.

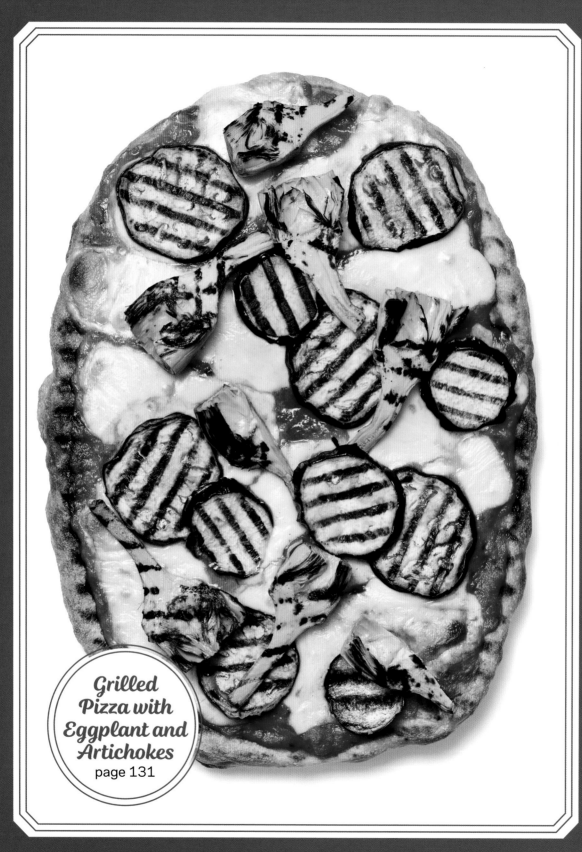

Grilled
Pizza with
Eggplant and
Artichokes
page 131

Grilled PIZZAS

Fire up the grill and take pizza night outside: These pies have great charred flavor and lots of fun toppings.

A fresh, crisp salad tastes great on top of grilled pizza.

Grilled White Pizza with Fennel Salad

ACTIVE: 30 min **|** TOTAL: 30 min **|** SERVES: 4

3 tablespoons extra-virgin olive oil, plus more for brushing
1 pound pizza dough, at room temperature (see page 15 or use store-bought)
4 ounces pancetta, diced (about ½ cup)
8 ounces asiago cheese, shredded (about 4 cups)
¼ cup grated parmesan cheese
1 small clove garlic, grated
1 small bulb fennel, trimmed, cored and thinly sliced
½ small head escarole, trimmed and thinly sliced
1 tablespoon balsamic vinegar
¼ to ½ teaspoon red pepper flakes
Kosher salt and freshly ground pepper

1. Preheat a grill to medium-high heat. Brush a baking sheet with olive oil. Form the pizza dough into a 9-by-12-inch oval on the baking sheet; cover loosely with plastic wrap and set aside.

2. Heat 1 tablespoon olive oil in a large skillet over medium heat. Add the pancetta and cook, stirring occasionally, until crisp, about 6 minutes. Transfer to a paper towel–lined plate to drain.

3. Combine the asiago, parmesan and garlic in a bowl; set aside. Brush the grill grates with olive oil. Generously brush the top of the dough with olive oil and place on the grill grates; grill until golden on the bottom, 4 to 5 minutes. Flip and continue grilling until marked, about 2 more minutes. Loosen the crust with a spatula, then top with the cheese mixture. Cover and cook until the cheese melts, 3 to 4 minutes. Transfer to a cutting board.

4. Meanwhile, toss the fennel, escarole, the remaining 2 tablespoons olive oil, the vinegar and red pepper flakes in a bowl; season with salt and pepper. Scatter the salad over the pizza and top with the pancetta; season with salt.

PRO TIPS

Prep your toppings first and bring them outside on a sheet pan—that way you can assemble the pie grillside.

A rustic shape is best for grilled pizza. The crust may get misshapen as you put it on the grill anyway.

Measure the oil and vinegar for dressing the salad—you don't want to overdo it or the crust could get soggy.

The key to keeping your basil green? Tear it just before using.

Grilled Pizza alla Vodka

ACTIVE: 35 min | TOTAL: 45 min | SERVES: 4

¾ cup boxed strained tomatoes
¼ cup vodka
1 small clove garlic, grated
Kosher salt
¼ cup heavy cream
1 tablespoon extra-virgin olive oil, plus more for the grill
All-purpose flour, for dusting
1 pound pizza dough, at room temperature (see page 15 or use store-bought)
8 ounces mozzarella cheese, sliced
Pinch of red pepper flakes
Torn fresh basil, for topping

1. Make the sauce: Combine the tomatoes, vodka, garlic and a pinch of salt in a medium saucepan. Bring to a simmer and cook, stirring occasionally, until slightly thickened and the alcohol is cooked off, about 10 minutes. Add the heavy cream and simmer 5 more minutes; season with salt.

2. Preheat a grill to medium-low to medium heat. Oil the grates.

3. Dust a large piece of parchment paper with flour, then dust the pizza dough with flour. Roll out the dough on the parchment into a rustic 10-by-14-inch oval or rectangle (about ⅛ inch thick). Drizzle the dough with the olive oil and rub all over.

4. Lift the parchment and flip the dough onto the grill; immediately remove the parchment. Grill, rotating the dough halfway through if needed, until slightly puffed on top and marked on the bottom, 3 to 5 minutes.

5. Remove the dough using tongs and flip onto a cutting board, cooked-side up. Top with the creamy tomato sauce, mozzarella and red pepper flakes. Slide the pizza back onto the grill. Cover and cook, rotating the pizza as needed, until the crust is well marked and the cheese is melted, 3 to 5 minutes. Remove to the cutting board and top with torn basil.

Grilled Pizza with Spinach and Kale

ACTIVE: 35 min **I** TOTAL: 35 min **I** SERVES: 4

2   tablespoons extra-virgin
     olive oil, plus more for
     the grill
2   cups baby spinach
2   cups chopped kale
Kosher salt and freshly
     ground pepper
All-purpose flour, for dusting
1   pound pizza dough, at room
     temperature (see page 15
     or use store-bought)
¼   cup pesto
8   ounces mozzarella
     cheese, sliced
1   cup frozen peas, thawed
Torn fresh mint, red pepper
     flakes and grated parmesan
     cheese, for topping

1. Preheat a grill to medium-low to medium heat. Oil the grates.

2. Heat 1 tablespoon olive oil in a large skillet over medium-high heat. Add the spinach and kale and cook, stirring, until wilted, about 2 minutes; season with salt and pepper.

3. Dust a large piece of parchment paper with flour, then dust the pizza dough with flour. Roll out the dough on the parchment into a rustic 10-by-14-inch oval or rectangle (about ⅛ inch thick). Drizzle the dough with the remaining 1 tablespoon olive oil and rub all over.

4. Lift the parchment and flip the dough onto the grill; immediately remove the parchment. Grill, rotating the dough halfway through if needed, until slightly puffed on top and marked on the bottom, 3 to 5 minutes.

5. Remove the dough using tongs and flip onto a cutting board, cooked-side up. Top with the pesto, mozzarella, peas and spinach-kale mixture. Slide the pizza back onto the grill. Cover and cook, rotating the pizza as needed, until the crust is well marked and the cheese is melted, 3 to 5 minutes. Remove to the cutting board; top with torn mint, red pepper flakes and parmesan.

Use store-bought pesto for this pizza or make your own on page 94.

Grilled Pizza with Pork and Pineapple

ACTIVE: 40 min | TOTAL: 40 min | SERVES: 4

Extra-virgin olive oil, for brushing
1   pound pizza dough (see
     page 15 or use store-bought)
1   pork tenderloin (about
     1¼ pounds), trimmed
Kosher salt and freshly ground
     pepper
⅓   cup teriyaki glaze
½   pineapple, peeled, cored
     and thinly sliced
1   red onion, sliced into thick
     rings
1½   cups shredded whole-milk
     mozzarella cheese
½   cup fresh cilantro

1. Preheat a grill to medium-high heat. Brush a baking sheet with olive oil. Place the pizza dough on the pan and turn to coat with the oil; set aside to bring to room temperature.

2. Slice the pork lengthwise down the center almost all the way through, then open like a book and flatten with your hands. Season the pork with salt and pepper and brush all over with 2 tablespoons teriyaki glaze. Brush the pineapple and onion slices with olive oil and season lightly with salt and pepper.

3. Brush the grill grates with olive oil. Arrange the pineapple and onion on one side of the grill and the pork on the other side. Grill the pineapple and onion until tender and lightly charred, 2 to 3 minutes per side; transfer to a plate. Grill the pork until cooked through, about 6 minutes per side; transfer to a cutting board.

4. Stretch the pizza dough into a 9-by-12-inch rectangle on the baking sheet. Reduce the grill heat to low; place the dough on the grill and cook until puffed on top and charred on the bottom, 1 to 2 minutes. Flip and top with the mozzarella. Cover and cook until the crust is cooked through and the cheese is melted, 2 to 3 minutes. Transfer to a cutting board. Cut the pineapple and pork into bite-size pieces; scatter over the crust along with the onion. Drizzle with the remaining teriyaki glaze and sprinkle with the cilantro.

PRO TIPS

Don't use cooking spray on a lit grill—it'll flare up. Instead, hold an oiled paper towel with tongs and rub the grates.

Pizza crust cooks quickly on the grill. Keep an eye on it and flip the crust as soon as it's puffed and charred.

Grill the pizza crust and the toppings too!

PRO TIP

Raw mushrooms contain a lot of moisture; it's best to precook them before topping your pizza.

Grilled Pizza with Mushrooms and Fontina

ACTIVE: 45 min **I** TOTAL: 45 min **I** SERVES: 4

3   tablespoons extra-virgin olive oil, plus more for the grill
2   tablespoons unsalted butter
12 ounces mixed mushrooms, diced
Kosher salt and freshly ground pepper
2   large cloves garlic, minced
4   teaspoons chopped fresh thyme
2   tablespoons sherry vinegar
4   ounces gruyère cheese, shredded
4   ounces fontina cheese, shredded
All-purpose flour, for dusting
1   pound pizza dough, at room temperature (see page 15 or use store-bought)
Chopped fresh chives, for topping

1. Preheat a grill to medium-low to medium heat. Oil the grates.

2. Heat 2 tablespoons olive oil and the butter in a large skillet over medium-high heat. Add the mushrooms and cook, stirring, until tender, about 6 minutes; season with salt and pepper. Add the garlic and thyme; cook 30 seconds. Remove from the heat and stir in the sherry vinegar. Combine the gruyère and fontina in a bowl.

3. Dust a large piece of parchment paper with flour, then dust the pizza dough with flour. Roll out the dough on the parchment into a rustic 10-by-14-inch oval or rectangle (about ⅛ inch thick). Drizzle the dough with the remaining 1 tablespoon olive oil and rub all over.

4. Lift the parchment and flip the dough onto the grill; immediately remove the parchment. Grill, rotating the dough halfway through if needed, until slightly puffed on top and marked on the bottom, 3 to 5 minutes.

5. Remove the dough using tongs and flip onto a cutting board, cooked-side up. Top with half of the cheese mixture, then the sautéed mushrooms, then the remaining cheese mixture. Slide the pizza back onto the grill. Cover and cook, rotating the pizza as needed, until the crust is well marked and the cheese is melted, 3 to 5 minutes. Remove to the cutting board and sprinkle with chopped chives.

Grilled Pizza with Hummus and Tomatoes

ACTIVE: 40 min | TOTAL: 40 min | SERVES: 4

¼ cup plus 1 tablespoon extra-virgin olive oil, plus more for the grill and for drizzling
¼ cup za'atar
All-purpose flour, for dusting
1 pound pizza dough, at room temperature (see page 15 or use store-bought)
4 ounces crumbled feta cheese
½ cup hummus
2 small tomatoes, sliced
Flaky salt, for sprinkling

1. Preheat a grill to medium-low to medium heat. Oil the grates.

2. Combine the za'atar and ¼ cup olive oil in a small bowl. Mix to make a paste.

3. Dust a large piece of parchment paper with flour, then dust the pizza dough with flour. Roll out the dough on the parchment into a rustic 10-by-14-inch oval or rectangle (about ⅛ inch thick). Drizzle the dough with the remaining 1 tablespoon olive oil and rub all over.

4. Lift the parchment and flip the dough onto the grill; immediately remove the parchment. Grill, rotating the dough halfway through if needed, until slightly puffed on top and marked on the bottom, 3 to 5 minutes.

5. Remove the dough using tongs and flip onto a cutting board, cooked-side up. Top with the spice paste and feta. Slide the pizza back onto the grill. Cover and cook, rotating the pizza as needed, until the crust is well marked and the cheese is soft, 3 to 5 minutes. Remove to the cutting board.

6. Mix the hummus and 2 tablespoons water in a small bowl. Drizzle onto the pizza and top with the tomatoes. Drizzle with olive oil and sprinkle with flaky salt.

PRO TIP

Serve any leftovers at room temperature—the hummus sauce and fresh tomatoes don't reheat well.

Grilled shrimp
is a tasty,
unexpected
topping!

Grilled Pizza with Shrimp and Feta

ACTIVE: 35 min **I** TOTAL: 35 min **I** SERVES: 4

¾   pound medium shrimp,
      peeled and deveined
1   red onion, sliced into rounds
¼   cup extra-virgin olive oil,
      plus more for brushing
½   teaspoon dried oregano
Kosher salt and freshly ground
      pepper
1   pound pizza dough, at room
      temperature (see page 15
      or use store-bought)
1   cup cherry or grape
      tomatoes, halved
½   cup crumbled feta cheese
2   tablespoons chopped fresh
      parsley

1. Preheat a grill to medium-high heat. Toss the shrimp and onion in a bowl with the olive oil and oregano. Season with salt and pepper.

2. Stretch the pizza dough into a rustic 8-by-10-inch rectangle. Lightly brush the grill with olive oil. Lay the dough on the grill and cook until the top begins to bubble and the bottom is marked, about 3 minutes. Remove with tongs and put cooked-side up on a cutting board. Brush with olive oil.

3. Grill the shrimp and onion, turning, until the onion softens and the shrimp are lightly charred, about 5 minutes; separate the onion rings. Top the crust with the shrimp and onion, then slide the pizza back onto the grill. Top with the tomatoes and feta, cover and grill until the dough is cooked through and the cheese is soft, about 5 more minutes.

4. Carefully transfer the pizza to the cutting board and sprinkle with the parsley.

PRO TIPS

If your grill grates are wide, thread the shrimp onto skewers to prevent them from falling through.

Slice the red onion into rounds, but don't separate the rings before grilling. Intact rounds are easier to flip.

Feta doesn't melt the same way other cheeses do. Grill the pie until the cheese is soft; don't wait for it to melt.

Put out toppings like avocado and pico de gallo and let guests top their own slice.

Grilled Pizza with Spicy Chorizo and Corn

ACTIVE: 35 min **I** TOTAL: 45 min **I** SERVES: 4

1   tablespoon extra-virgin olive oil, plus more for the grill
2   ears of corn, shucked
½   cup pizza sauce
2   canned chipotle chiles in adobo sauce, minced
All-purpose flour, for dusting
1   pound pizza dough, at room temperature (see page 15 or use store-bought)
8   ounces fresh chorizo, cooked and crumbled
1   8-ounce bag shredded Mexican cheese blend
Diced avocado and/or pico de gallo, for topping

1. Preheat a grill to medium heat. Oil the grates.

2. Grill the corn, turning, until charred, 8 to 10 minutes. Stand the cobs upright in a bowl and cut off the kernels. Mix the pizza sauce and chipotles in a small bowl.

3. Dust a large piece of parchment paper with flour, then dust the pizza dough with flour. Roll out the dough on the parchment into a rustic 10-by-14-inch oval or rectangle (about ⅛ inch thick). Drizzle the dough with the olive oil and rub all over.

4. Lift the parchment and flip the dough onto the grill; immediately remove the parchment. Grill, rotating the dough halfway through if needed, until slightly puffed on top and marked on the bottom, 3 to 5 minutes.

5. Remove the dough using tongs and flip onto a cutting board, cooked-side up. Top with the sauce, chorizo, corn and cheese. Slide the pizza back onto the grill. Cover and cook, rotating the pizza as needed, until the crust is well marked and the cheese is melted, 3 to 5 minutes. Remove to the cutting board and top with avocado and/or pico de gallo.

Grilled White Pizza with Garlic

ACTIVE: 35 min I TOTAL: 45 min I SERVES: 4

1 cup heavy cream
1 clove garlic, smashed
2 teaspoons unsalted butter, at room temperature
2 teaspoons all-purpose flour, plus more for dusting
Kosher salt and freshly ground pepper
1 tablespoon extra-virgin olive oil, plus more for the grill
All-purpose flour, for dusting
1 pound pizza dough, at room temperature (see page 15 or use store-bought)
1 8-ounce bag shredded mozzarella cheese
¼ cup grated parmesan cheese
Dried oregano, for topping

1. Combine the heavy cream and garlic in a small saucepan. Bring to a simmer over medium-low heat and cook, stirring occasionally, until slightly thickened, about 12 minutes.

2. Mix the butter and flour in a small bowl until combined. Whisk the mixture into the warm cream and cook until thickened, about 30 seconds; season with salt and pepper. Discard the garlic.

3. Preheat a grill to medium-low to medium heat. Oil the grates.

4. Dust a large piece of parchment paper with flour, then dust the pizza dough with flour. Roll out the dough on the parchment into a rustic 10-by-14-inch oval or rectangle (about ⅛ inch thick). Drizzle the dough with the olive oil and rub all over.

5. Lift the parchment and flip the dough onto the grill; immediately remove the parchment. Grill, rotating the dough halfway through if needed, until slightly puffed on top and marked on the bottom, 3 to 5 minutes.

6. Remove the dough using tongs and flip onto a cutting board, cooked-side up. Top with the cream sauce, mozzarella and parmesan. Slide the pizza back onto the grill. Cover and cook, rotating the pizza as needed, until the crust is well marked and the cheese is melted, 3 to 5 minutes. Remove to the cutting board and top with dried oregano.

PRO TIP

Grills can have hot spots. Keep an eye on the crust and rotate the pizza as needed so it's evenly charred.

Sometimes all you need is cheese!

Grilled Pizza with Summer Squash

ACTIVE: 35 min I TOTAL: 35 min I SERVES: 4

½ red onion, very thinly sliced
Juice of ½ lemon
Kosher salt
1 pound pizza dough, at room temperature (see page 15 or use store-bought)
All-purpose flour, for dusting
2 large or 3 medium zucchini and/or yellow squash, sliced ¼ inch thick on an angle
5 tablespoons extra-virgin olive oil
¼ teaspoon red pepper flakes
2 tablespoons plus 1 teaspoon za'atar
1½ cups shredded low-moisture mozzarella cheese
½ cup crumbled feta cheese
1 cup chopped fresh cilantro

1. Preheat a grill to medium heat. Combine the red onion, lemon juice and a big pinch of salt in a medium bowl; toss well. Cut the pizza dough into 4 pieces. On a lightly floured surface, press one piece of dough with your fingertips to make a 4- to 5-inch round, then roll out into an 8-inch round. Repeat with the remaining dough.

2. Combine the zucchini and/or yellow squash, 2 tablespoons olive oil, ¾ teaspoon salt and the red pepper flakes in a large bowl; toss well to coat. Grill until well marked and tender, 2 to 3 minutes per side. Remove to a plate.

3. Combine 2 tablespoons za'atar, a pinch of salt and the remaining 3 tablespoons olive oil in a small bowl. Grill the dough rounds until they are marked on the bottom and start bubbling up in spots, about 3 minutes. Flip the dough, brush with the za'atar oil and top with the mozzarella and zucchini and/or yellow squash. Cook until the dough is marked on the bottom and the mozzarella melts, about 3 minutes.

4. Remove each pizza to a plate, scatter the feta and red onion on top and sprinkle with the remaining 1 teaspoon za'atar, a pinch of salt and the cilantro.

PRO TIPS

Cut the zucchini and/or yellow squash diagonally; you'll get more surface area for grilling, plus the slices won't fall through the grates.

Raw red onion can taste harsh. To mellow it out, slice the onion, then toss with lemon juice and set aside; the onion will start to pickle.

Everyone gets an individual-size pie!

PRO TIP

Roll out the dough on floured parchment paper, then use the parchment to help you flip the dough onto the grill.

Grilled Pizza with Peaches and Burrata

ACTIVE: 35 min **I** TOTAL: 45 min **I** SERVES: 4

1   cup heavy cream
1   clove garlic, smashed
2   teaspoons unsalted butter, at room temperature
2   teaspoons all-purpose flour, plus more for dusting
Kosher salt and freshly ground pepper
1   tablespoon extra-virgin olive oil, plus more for the grill
1   pound pizza dough, at room temperature (see page 15 or use store-bought)
8   ounces burrata cheese, torn
2   peaches, thinly sliced
Thinly sliced speck, for topping

1. Combine the heavy cream and garlic in a small saucepan. Bring to a simmer over medium-low heat and cook, stirring occasionally, until slightly thickened, about 12 minutes.

2. Mix the butter and flour in a small bowl until combined. Whisk the mixture into the warm cream and cook until thickened, about 30 seconds; season with salt and pepper. Discard the garlic.

3. Preheat a grill to medium-low to medium heat. Oil the grates.

4. Dust a large piece of parchment paper with flour, then dust the pizza dough with flour. Roll out the dough on the parchment into a rustic 10-by-14-inch oval or rectangle (about ⅛ inch thick). Drizzle the dough with the olive oil and rub all over.

5. Lift the parchment and flip the dough onto the grill; immediately remove the parchment. Grill, rotating the dough halfway through if needed, until slightly puffed on top and marked on the bottom, 3 to 5 minutes.

6. Remove the dough using tongs and flip onto a cutting board, cooked-side up. Top with the cream sauce, burrata and peaches. Slide the pizza back onto the grill. Cover and cook, rotating the pizza as needed, until the crust is well marked and the cheese is melted, 3 to 5 minutes. Remove to the cutting board and top with speck.

Grilled Ranch Pizza with Bacon and Broccoli

ACTIVE: 35 min **I** TOTAL: 45 min **I** SERVES: 4

3 cups small broccoli florets
3 scallions, light parts sliced into ½-inch pieces and dark greens thinly sliced
2 tablespoons extra-virgin olive oil, plus more for the grill
Kosher salt and freshly ground pepper
All-purpose flour, for dusting
1 pound pizza dough, at room temperature (see page 15 or use store-bought)
½ cup ranch dressing
1 8-ounce bag shredded mozzarella cheese
½ cup crumbled cooked thick-cut bacon

1. Preheat a grill to medium-low to medium heat. Preheat a grill basket on top of the grill.

2. Toss the broccoli, light scallion parts and 1 tablespoon olive oil in a large bowl; season with salt and pepper. Transfer to the preheated grill basket and grill until the vegetables are charred and crisp-tender, 5 to 8 minutes.

3. Dust a large piece of parchment paper with flour, then dust the pizza dough with flour. Roll out the dough on the parchment into a rustic 10-by-14-inch oval or rectangle (about ⅛ inch thick). Drizzle the dough with the remaining 1 tablespoon olive oil and rub all over.

4. Lift the parchment and flip the dough onto the grill; immediately remove the parchment. Grill, rotating the dough halfway through if needed, until slightly puffed on top and marked on the bottom, 3 to 5 minutes.

5. Remove the dough using tongs and flip onto a cutting board, cooked-side up. Top with the ranch dressing, mozzarella, bacon and grilled vegetables. Slide the pizza back onto the grill. Cover and cook, rotating the pizza as needed, until the crust is well marked and the cheese is melted, 3 to 5 minutes. Remove to the cutting board and top with the scallion greens.

PRO TIP

Use a grill basket to grill broccoli florets and other small veggies.

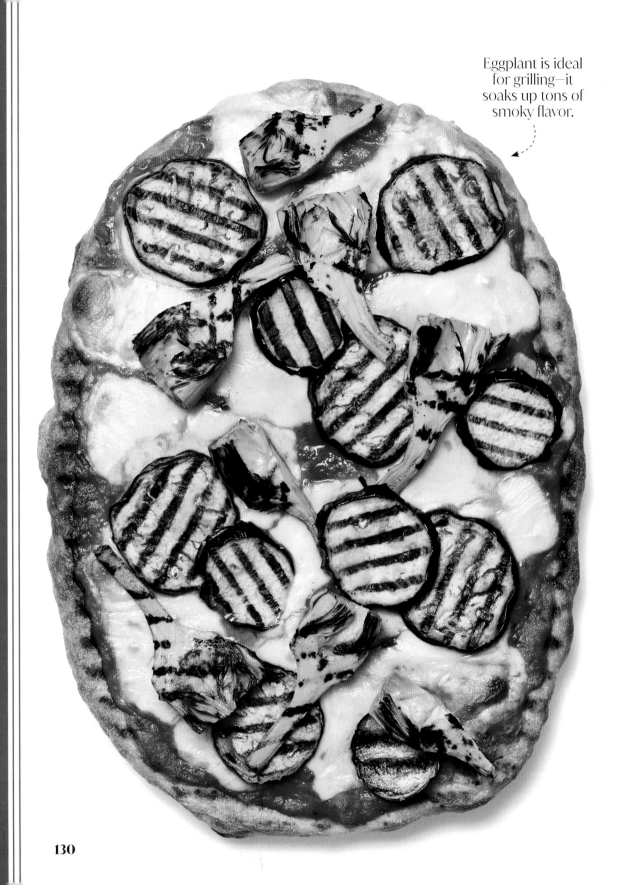

Eggplant is ideal for grilling—it soaks up tons of smoky flavor.

Grilled Pizza with Eggplant and Artichokes

ACTIVE: 45 min I TOTAL: 45 min I SERVES: 4

3 tablespoons extra-virgin olive oil, plus more for brushing
2 cloves garlic, smashed
1 28-ounce can whole peeled tomatoes, crushed by hand
1 sprig basil, plus torn basil leaves for topping
Pinch of sugar
Kosher salt and freshly ground pepper
1 small eggplant, cut into ¼- to ½-inch-thick rounds
1 6-ounce jar marinated artichoke hearts, drained
All-purpose flour, for dusting
1 pound pizza dough, at room temperature (see page 15 or use store-bought)
8 ounces mozzarella cheese, sliced

1. Preheat a grill to medium-low to medium heat on one side and medium-high heat on the other. Brush the grill grates with olive oil.

2. Make the sauce: Heat 2 tablespoons olive oil and the garlic in a saucepan over medium-high heat until sizzling. Add the tomatoes, basil sprig and sugar; season with salt and pepper. Simmer, stirring, until thickened, 15 to 20 minutes. Discard the basil and garlic.

3. Meanwhile, brush the eggplant with olive oil and season with salt and pepper. Grill the artichoke hearts and eggplant over medium-high heat, flipping, until the artichokes are lightly charred and the eggplant is tender, 2 to 3 minutes for the artichokes and 8 to 10 minutes for the eggplant.

4. Dust a large piece of parchment paper with flour, then dust the pizza dough with flour. Roll out the dough on the parchment into a rustic 10-by-14-inch oval or rectangle (about ⅛ inch thick). Drizzle the dough with the remaining 1 tablespoon olive oil and rub all over.

5. Lift the parchment and flip the dough onto the grill over medium-low to medium heat; immediately remove the parchment. Grill, rotating the dough halfway through if needed, until slightly puffed on top and marked on the bottom, 3 to 5 minutes.

6. Remove the dough using tongs and flip onto a cutting board, cooked-side up. Top with the tomato sauce, mozzarella and grilled vegetables. Slide the pizza back onto the grill. Cover and cook, rotating the pizza as needed, until the crust is well marked and the cheese is melted, 3 to 5 minutes. Remove to the cutting board and top with torn basil.

Heirloom
Tomato
Puff Pastry
Pizza
page 147

Alternative PITTZAS

Skip the usual dough
and try a new kind of pie:
These are made with pita,
French bread, puff pastry,
tortillas and more.

Don't toss your carrot greens! Use them to make this pesto.

Tahini-Carrot Puff Pastry Pizza

ACTIVE: 45 min I TOTAL: 1½ hr I SERVES: 6 to 8

⅓   cup raw cashews
12 ounces baby carrots (3 to 4 bunches), trimmed and sliced in half lengthwise if large, plus ¼ cup chopped carrot greens (or use parsley)
¼   cup fresh cilantro, plus more for topping
2   tablespoons tahini
1   tablespoon white wine vinegar
¼   cup plus 1 tablespoon fresh orange juice
Pinch of smoked paprika
Kosher salt and freshly ground pepper
1   sheet frozen puff pastry (half of a 17-ounce package), thawed
1   large egg, lightly beaten
1   tablespoon extra-virgin olive oil
1   teaspoon whole coriander seeds, finely crushed
1   teaspoon sugar

1. Preheat the oven to 425°. Put the cashews in a bowl and cover with hot water. Let soak until softened, 30 to 45 minutes; drain.

2. Puree the cashews in a blender with the carrot greens, cilantro, 2 tablespoons cold water, the tahini, vinegar, 1 tablespoon orange juice, the paprika, ½ teaspoon salt, a few grinds of pepper and a few ice cubes, scraping down the sides often, until very smooth. Refrigerate until ready to use.

3. Roll out the puff pastry into an 11-inch square on a sheet of parchment paper. Slide the dough (on the parchment) onto a baking sheet. Score a ½-inch border around the edge of the dough with a paring knife. Brush the border with the beaten egg. Prick the center of the dough all over with a fork.

4. Bake the dough until golden, 10 to 12 minutes. Remove from the oven, prick the center of the dough with a paring knife and gently press with the bottom of a measuring cup to flatten. Return to the oven and bake until golden brown, 8 to 10 more minutes. Let cool. Gently flatten inside the border again, if necessary.

5. Toss the carrots with the olive oil, coriander seeds, ½ teaspoon salt and a few grinds of pepper on a rimmed baking sheet. Roast, stirring once, until tender, 15 to 20 minutes. Let cool.

6. Simmer the remaining ¼ cup orange juice and the sugar in a small skillet over medium heat until syrupy, about 3 minutes. Spread the cashew sauce on the cooled crust and arrange the carrots on top. Brush the orange syrup over the carrots. Top with cilantro.

PRO TIPS

Thaw puff pastry overnight in the refrigerator or let it thaw on the countertop; don't microwave.

A beaten egg gives puff pastry a nice sheen; brush it onto the exposed crust before baking.

Ham and Cheese Pie with Artichokes and Broccoli

ACTIVE: 30 min I TOTAL: 40 min I SERVES: 4

1 tablespoon extra-virgin olive oil, plus more for brushing
1 9-ounce box frozen artichoke hearts
1 small leek (white and light green parts only), sliced
1 4-ounce piece Black Forest ham, chopped
1½ cups chopped broccoli florets
Kosher salt and freshly ground pepper
1 round refrigerated pie dough (half of a 14-ounce package)
1 tablespoon dijon mustard
1 cup grated gruyère cheese

1. Preheat the oven to 450°. Heat the olive oil in a large nonstick skillet over medium-high heat. Add the artichoke hearts in a single layer and cook, turning, until browned, 2 to 3 minutes. Scatter the leek, ham and broccoli on top and cook, stirring, until the vegetables soften, 2 to 3 minutes; season with salt and pepper.

2. Line a rimmed baking sheet with foil. Unroll the pie dough on the prepared pan and gently flatten any curled edges. Spread the mustard on the dough, leaving a 1-inch border. Top with half the gruyère, then the vegetable mixture, then the remaining gruyère.

3. Fold in the edge of the dough, pleating as needed. Lightly brush the crust with olive oil and sprinkle with pepper. Bake until the pastry is golden brown and the cheese melts, 20 to 25 minutes.

PRO TIPS

Leeks can have a lot of dirt and sand on the inside. To clean them, slice them first, then wash in a salad spinner with cold water.

Keep a box of frozen artichokes on hand for recipes like this one. They taste more like fresh than the canned stuff.

Assemble this pie like a galette: Spread all the toppings in the middle of the dough, then fold in the edge, pleating as you go.

Refrigerated pie dough is the secret to this easy dinner.

----Serve this pizza
for brunch!

Smoked Salmon Puff Pastry Pizza

ACTIVE: 45 min | TOTAL: 1 hr | SERVES: 6 to 8

1   sheet frozen puff pastry (half of a 17-ounce package), thawed
1   large egg
¼   cup heavy cream, plus more for the egg wash
1   bunch radishes, trimmed and thinly sliced (about 1½ cups)
1   5-ounce package garlic-herb cheese spread (such as Boursin), at room temperature
2   tablespoons champagne vinegar
1   tablespoon finely chopped fresh tarragon
1   tablespoon finely chopped fresh parsley
Kosher salt
2   ounces smoked salmon, torn into pieces
Flaky sea salt

1. Preheat the oven to 400°. Roll out the puff pastry into an 11-inch square on a sheet of parchment paper. Slide the dough (on the parchment) onto a baking sheet. Beat the egg with a splash of heavy cream. Brush a 1-inch border of the egg wash around the edges of the dough, then fold in each side about ½ inch to make a thin border and press to seal. Prick the center of the dough all over with a fork, then brush all over with the egg wash.

2. Bake the dough until crisp and golden brown, about 25 minutes. Prick the center of the dough with a paring knife and gently press with the bottom of a measuring cup to flatten, if necessary. Remove to a rack and let cool.

3. Meanwhile, soak the sliced radishes in a large bowl of ice water until crisp and just starting to curl, about 15 minutes; drain and pat dry with paper towels.

4. Mix the garlic-herb cheese spread and heavy cream in a medium bowl until smooth. Whisk the vinegar, tarragon, parsley and a pinch of kosher salt in a large bowl. Add the radishes and smoked salmon and toss to coat.

5. Spread the cheese mixture on the cooled crust, then pile the radishes and smoked salmon on top. Sprinkle with flaky sea salt.

PRO TIPS

Bake the crust a few hours ahead, then add your toppings before serving. The pie tastes best at room temperature.

For extra flavor, sprinkle everything seasoning on top of the pie before serving.

Lavash Pizzas with Arugula and Prosciutto

ACTIVE: 20 min **I** TOTAL: 20 min **I** SERVES: 4

2   pieces lavash, halved
1   tablespoon extra-virgin olive oil, plus more for brushing
½   cup grated fontina cheese (about 2 ounces)
4   ounces thinly sliced prosciutto, torn
4   cups baby arugula
1   bulb fennel, halved, cored and thinly sliced
2   tablespoons roughly chopped fresh parsley
½   red onion, thinly sliced
2   tablespoons balsamic vinegar
Kosher salt and freshly ground pepper
½   cup crumbled gorgonzola or other blue cheese (about 2 ounces)

1. Preheat a grill to medium heat. Lightly brush the lavash with olive oil, then grill until marked on the bottom, about 2 minutes. Flip the bread and immediately top with the fontina. Continue grilling until the cheese melts, about 2 minutes. Transfer to a platter and top with the prosciutto.

2. Combine the arugula, fennel, parsley and red onion in a large bowl. Drizzle with the vinegar and 1 tablespoon olive oil; season with salt and pepper and then toss. Pile on top of the pizzas and sprinkle with the gorgonzola.

PRO TIPS

Lavash is a good size for these pizzas, but you can use any kind of flatbread or pita.

Use a mandoline to thinly slice tough veggies like fennel or cabbage.

If you're not a blue cheese fan, go with crumbled goat cheese instead. Or top the pie with dollops of ricotta.

140

This pizza is ready in just 20 minutes!

It's breakfast
for dinner!

Bacon-and-Egg Puff Pastry Pizzas

ACTIVE: 15 min I TOTAL: 25 min I SERVES: 4

All-purpose flour, for dusting
1   sheet frozen puff pastry
      (half of a 17-ounce
      package), thawed
2   slices bacon
1½   cups shredded havarti
      cheese
3   tablespoons shredded
      parmesan cheese
4   large eggs
Kosher salt and freshly ground
      pepper
Chopped fresh chives,
      for topping

1. Preheat the oven to 425°. Line 2 baking sheets with parchment paper. On a lightly floured surface, roll out the puff pastry into a 12-inch square, then cut into 4 equal squares. Slightly fold in and pinch the edges of each square to form 4 rounds. Transfer to the prepared baking sheets and prick all over with a fork. Bake until golden, 8 to 10 minutes.

2. Meanwhile, cook the bacon in a medium skillet over medium heat, turning, until crisp, 8 to 10 minutes. Transfer to paper towels to drain, then crumble.

3. Let the crusts cool slightly on the baking sheets. If the centers are very puffy, prick with a fork to deflate. Sprinkle evenly with the havarti and parmesan. Make a shallow well in the cheese in the center of each pizza and crack an egg into each well; season with salt and pepper. Top with the bacon, then return to the oven and bake until the egg whites are set, 10 to 15 minutes. Top with chopped chives.

PRO TIPS

Prick the puff pastry all over with a fork before baking to prevent it from puffing up too much in the oven.

Make a well in the grated cheese on each pizza to hold the egg; this will keep the egg from overflowing.

Remove the pizzas from the oven when the eggs are done. The whites should be set, but the yolks can still be runny.

Tortilla Pizzas with Chorizo

ACTIVE: 30 min | TOTAL: 30 min | SERVES: 4

2 tablespoons extra-virgin olive oil
8 ounces fresh chorizo, casings removed, crumbled
4 8-inch flour tortillas
1 16-ounce can refried beans
1 cup shredded Oaxacan cheese (about 4 ounces)
3 ounces mâche lettuce or arugula
½ cup fresh cilantro
3 radishes, thinly sliced
1 red jalapeño pepper, sliced (remove seeds for less heat)
Juice of 1 lime
Kosher salt
1 avocado, diced
⅓ cup crema or sour cream

1. Preheat the oven to 400°. Heat 1 tablespoon olive oil in a large nonstick skillet over medium heat. Add the chorizo and cook, stirring occasionally, until browned, about 4 minutes. Remove the chorizo to a plate with a slotted spoon. Transfer all but 1 tablespoon of the drippings to a small bowl; stir the remaining 1 tablespoon olive oil into the bowl (reserve the skillet). Divide the tortillas between 2 baking sheets and brush the tops with the drippings mixture. Bake until the tortillas are crisp and lightly golden, about 5 minutes.

2. Heat the skillet with the reserved 1 tablespoon drippings over medium-high heat. Add the refried beans and cook, stirring, until they're warm and spreadable, about 2 minutes. Spread the beans on the tortillas and sprinkle with the chorizo and cheese. Bake until the cheese melts, about 5 minutes.

3. Meanwhile, combine the lettuce, cilantro, radishes, jalapeño and lime juice in a large bowl; season with salt and toss. Top each tortilla with the salad, avocado and crema.

PRO TIPS

Be sure to crisp up your tortillas in the oven before adding the toppings—otherwise the tortillas may get soggy.

Oaxacan cheese melts well and becomes very stretchy. You can use mozzarella as a substitute.

Crema is great for drizzling, but sour cream is too thick. Thin it out with a squeeze of lemon or lime juice, or a little water.

Pile on your favorite taco toppings!

Summer is the perfect time for a fresh tomato pie!

Heirloom Tomato Puff Pastry Pizza

ACTIVE: 25 min **I** TOTAL: 45 min **I** SERVES: 6

1   sheet frozen puff pastry
     (half of a 17-ounce
     package), thawed
All-purpose flour, for dusting
1   8-ounce package cream
     cheese, at room temperature
⅓   cup sour cream
½   teaspoon finely grated
     lemon zest, plus 1 teaspoon
     fresh lemon juice
¼   teaspoon sugar
Kosher salt and freshly ground
     pepper
2   tablespoons finely chopped
     fresh chives, plus more
     for topping
12   ounces assorted small
     heirloom tomatoes, halved

1. Preheat the oven to 400°. Unfold the puff pastry onto a floured piece of parchment paper and roll out into a 9-by-11-inch rectangle. Score ½ inch in from the edge, all the way around, using a paring knife. Slide the pastry (on the parchment) onto a baking sheet. Prick the center all over with a fork, then bake until golden brown, 20 to 25 minutes. Transfer to a rack to cool completely.

2. Meanwhile, combine the cream cheese, sour cream, lemon zest, lemon juice, sugar, ½ teaspoon salt and a few grinds of pepper in a large bowl and beat with a mixer on medium speed until smooth; stir in the chives. Spread the cream cheese mixture evenly on the cooled crust. Arrange the tomatoes on top; season with salt and pepper and top with more chives.

PRO TIPS

If your puff pastry starts to crack as you unfold it, it's probably not fully thawed. Let it sit at room temperature for a bit longer.

To create a raised edge, score a border all the way around the puff pastry with a paring knife, then prick the center with a fork.

Kitchen shears are great for cutting herbs; you can snip chives directly onto your pizza.

Cauliflower-Crust Pizza with Mushrooms

ACTIVE: 40 min **I** TOTAL: 50 min **I** SERVES: 2 to 4

1   1¼-pound head cauliflower, cut into florets
⅓   cup grated parmesan cheese
6   tablespoons potato starch
1   large egg, beaten
Kosher salt
1   teaspoon garlic powder
1   teaspoon onion powder
3   tablespoons extra-virgin olive oil
¾   pound cremini mushrooms, sliced
Freshly ground pepper
½   cup ricotta cheese
1   cup shredded mozzarella cheese (about 4 ounces)
Chopped fresh chives, for topping

1. Put a pizza stone or inverted baking sheet on the middle oven rack and preheat to 475°.

2. Pulse the cauliflower florets in a food processor until very finely chopped. Transfer to a clean kitchen towel and squeeze out any excess water. Transfer to a large bowl and stir in the parmesan, potato starch, beaten egg, 1 teaspoon salt, the garlic powder and onion powder. Turn out the mixture onto a piece of parchment paper and press into a thin 12-inch round.

3. Slide the crust (on the parchment) onto the hot pizza stone or baking sheet. Bake until golden, about 20 minutes.

4. Meanwhile, heat the olive oil in a large nonstick skillet over medium-high heat. Add the mushrooms, season with salt and pepper and cook, undisturbed, until golden brown on the bottom, about 5 minutes. Stir and cook until crisp in spots and golden brown all over, about 5 more minutes.

5. Put the ricotta in a small bowl and season with salt and pepper. Top the cauliflower crust with the seasoned ricotta, mozzarella and sautéed mushrooms. Return to the oven and bake until the mozzarella melts, about 5 minutes. Top with chives.

PRO TIPS

Be sure to squeeze the liquid out of the cauliflower after you chop it. Excess moisture will prevent the crust from getting crispy.

Potato starch acts as a binder in this crust; you can substitute flour, but then the crust won't be gluten-free.

Don't try rolling out this "dough"—just press it with your hands until you have a rough round.

This crust is totally gluten-free!

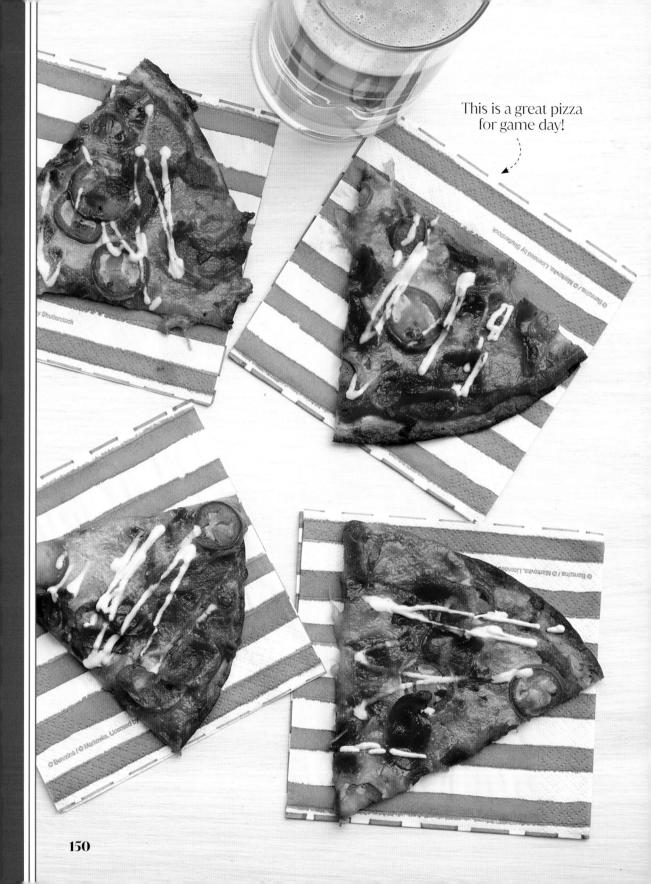

This is a great pizza for game day!

Jalapeño Popper Tortilla Pizzas

ACTIVE: 35 min **|** TOTAL: 55 min **|** SERVES: 6 to 8

1 teaspoon vegetable oil
10 slices bacon
4 burrito-size flour tortillas
1 cup pizza sauce
3 cups shredded mozzarella cheese (about 12 ounces)
½ cup pickled jalapeño slices, plus 2 teaspoons brine
2 ounces cream cheese
Kosher salt and freshly ground pepper

1. Preheat the oven to 500˚. Set a wire rack on each of 2 rimmed baking sheets. Heat the vegetable oil and bacon in a large nonstick skillet over medium-high heat. Cook, turning occasionally, until crisp, 8 to 10 minutes. Transfer the bacon to paper towels to drain, then chop. Pour the drippings into a small bowl and wipe out the skillet.

2. Return the skillet to medium-high heat. Lightly brush 1 tortilla with the reserved bacon drippings. Add to the skillet and cook until lightly browned on the bottom, about 2 minutes. Flip and cook, rotating the tortilla and gently pressing it with a spatula, until crisp, about 3 minutes. Transfer to one of the racks, crisp-side down. Repeat with the remaining tortillas and bacon drippings, reducing the heat if the tortillas are browning too quickly.

3. Spread the pizza sauce on the tortillas, then sprinkle with the mozzarella, chopped bacon and pickled jalapeños. Working in batches, bake the pizzas, 1 baking sheet at a time, until the cheese is melted and bubbling, about 8 minutes.

4. Microwave the cream cheese in a small microwave-safe bowl until runny, about 30 seconds. Stir in the jalapeño brine and season with salt and pepper. Drizzle on the pizzas.

PRO TIPS

To keep the bottoms of the tortillas crisp, bake these pizzas on a rack set on a baking sheet so the heat can circulate underneath.

Don't throw away the brine from a can of pickled jalapeños! It's great for dressings and sauces, like this cream cheese drizzle.

Asparagus-Beet Puff Pastry Pizza

ACTIVE: 45 min **|** TOTAL: 2 hr 15 min **|** SERVES: 6 to 8

3   small beets
2   tablespoons unsalted butter
1   onion, halved and thinly sliced
2   teaspoons chopped fresh lemon thyme (or regular thyme)
Kosher salt and freshly ground pepper
1   sheet frozen puff pastry (half of a 17-ounce package), thawed
1   large egg, lightly beaten
½   bunch thin asparagus, trimmed and cut into 3-inch pieces
2   tablespoons extra-virgin olive oil
2   ounces goat cheese, crumbled
1   tablespoon chopped fresh chives

1. Preheat the oven to 425°. Put the beets in a small baking dish and add about ½ inch water. Cover with foil and bake until the beets are easily pierced with the tip of a knife, 1 to 1½ hours. Transfer the beets to a plate and let cool. Wipe off the skins with a paper towel and slice into small wedges; set aside.

2. Meanwhile, heat the butter in a medium skillet over medium heat. Add the onion, 2 tablespoons water, 1 teaspoon thyme, a big pinch of salt and a few grinds of pepper and cook, stirring occasionally, until the onion is tender and caramelized, 20 to 25 minutes. (Add 1 to 2 teaspoons more water to the skillet, if needed.) Transfer the onion mixture to a food processor and puree until smooth. Let cool.

3. Roll out the puff pastry into a 9-by-11-inch rectangle on a sheet of parchment paper. Slide the dough (on the parchment) onto a baking sheet. Score a 1-inch border around the edge of the dough with a paring knife. Brush the border with the beaten egg. Spread the onion puree inside the border.

4. Combine the beets, asparagus, olive oil, the remaining 1 teaspoon thyme, ½ teaspoon salt and a few grinds of pepper in a bowl and toss to coat. Arrange on top of the onion puree.

5. Bake until the dough is well browned and the asparagus is tender, 30 to 35 minutes. Scatter the goat cheese and chives on top.

PRO TIPS

Caramelized onions are best cooked low and slow. Keep an eye on them; if they start to brown too quickly, reduce the heat.

If you can find lemon thyme, use it—it adds a great citrusy flavor. Regular thyme is a fine substitute.

You can serve this pie straight out of the oven, or let it cool and serve at room temperature.

Use frozen cauliflower crust for this shortcut pizza.

Cauliflower-Crust Pizzas with Artichokes

ACTIVE: 25 min I TOTAL: 25 min I SERVES: 4

2   10-inch frozen cauliflower
      crusts (6 to 8 ounces each)
1   tablespoon plus
      2 teaspoons extra-virgin
      olive oil
½   cup pizza sauce
1   cup shredded part-skim
      low-moisture mozzarella
      cheese (about 4 ounces)
¼   cup grated parmesan
      cheese
½   teaspoon dried oregano
½   cup quartered artichoke
      hearts packed in water,
      drained and roughly chopped
1   small head escarole,
      light green inner leaves only,
      roughly chopped
1   ounce mortadella, thinly
      sliced and chopped
1   jarred roasted red pepper,
      sliced
½   cup giardiniera, chopped,
      plus 1 tablespoon brine
Freshly ground pepper

1. Position racks in the upper and lower thirds of the oven; preheat to 425°. Put each cauliflower crust on a baking sheet. Brush each with 1 teaspoon olive oil.

2. Divide the pizza sauce between the crusts and spread almost to the edge with the back of a spoon. Sprinkle with the mozzarella, parmesan and oregano. Scatter the artichokes evenly over the pizzas.

3. Bake, switching the pans halfway through, until the crusts are crisp and the cheese browns slightly, 12 to 15 minutes.

4. Meanwhile, combine the escarole, mortadella, roasted pepper and giardiniera in a large bowl. Drizzle with the giardiniera brine and remaining 1 tablespoon olive oil and season with pepper. Toss. Serve the pizzas with the salad.

PRO TIPS

Measure your sauce and don't go overboard—cauliflower crust isn't sturdy enough to handle lots of sauce and toppings.

Switch the position of the baking sheets halfway through cooking to ensure that the crusts crisp up evenly.

Grilled Pita Pizzas with Tomatoes, Olives and Arugula

ACTIVE: 30 min **I** TOTAL: 30 min **I** SERVES: 4

3   medium tomatoes
1   tablespoon extra-virgin olive oil, plus more for brushing and drizzling
Kosher salt and freshly ground pepper
3   cups baby arugula
½   cup pitted kalamata olives, roughly chopped
1   tablespoon fresh rosemary, roughly chopped
1   large red onion, cut into 1-inch-thick rounds
4   6- to 8-inch pocketless pitas
½   cup ricotta cheese
¼   pound part-skim mozzarella cheese, diced
Pinch of red pepper flakes

1. Core the tomatoes and halve them crosswise, then squeeze the juices and seeds into a large bowl. Whisk in 1 tablespoon olive oil and season with salt and pepper. Add the arugula but don't toss; set aside. Dice the tomatoes and toss in a separate bowl with the olives and rosemary.

2. Preheat a grill to medium-high heat. Brush the onion rounds with olive oil and season with salt. Grill until soft, 3 to 4 minutes per side. Transfer to a plate and separate the rings. Reduce the grill heat to medium.

3. Brush both sides of the pitas with olive oil and grill until marked, 2 to 3 minutes per side. Top with some of the tomato-olive mixture, ricotta, mozzarella and onion. Cover and grill until the cheese melts, 2 to 3 minutes.

4. Toss the arugula with the dressing and pile on top of the pitas. Season with salt and the red pepper flakes and drizzle with olive oil.

PRO TIPS

Pocketless pitas make great pizza crusts—they're thicker and sturdier than regular pitas.

You can also make these pizzas indoors: Use a grill pan to toast the pitas, then bake at 400˚ to melt the cheese.

It's pizza and
salad in one!

Pizza + lasagna
= pizzagna!

PRO TIPS

Line the pan with foil and leave an overhang. You can use the excess foil to lift the pizzagna out of the pan after baking.

If the top starts browning too quickly, tent the pan with foil and continue baking.

Pepperoni Pizzagna

ACTIVE: 1 hr **I** TOTAL: 2½ hr **I** SERVES: 8

3   tablespoons extra-virgin olive oil, plus more for the pan
4   button mushrooms, sliced
Kosher salt and freshly ground pepper
8   ounces sweet Italian sausage, casings removed
1   small red onion, finely chopped
1   small green bell pepper, finely chopped
1   24-ounce jar marinara sauce
½   cup roughly chopped deli-sliced ham (about 2 ounces)
¼   cup pitted black olives, sliced
1   cup sliced pepperoni (about 3 ounces)
16 lasagna noodles
3   cups shredded part-skim mozzarella cheese (about 12 ounces)
1   8-ounce container whole-milk ricotta cheese
½   cup grated parmesan cheese (about 1 ounce)
2   large eggs, lightly beaten

1. Heat 2 tablespoons olive oil in a large pot over medium-high heat. Add the mushrooms, season with salt and pepper and cook, stirring, until lightly browned, about 5 minutes. Transfer to a plate using a slotted spoon. Add the sausage to the pot and cook, breaking up the meat, until no longer pink, about 3 minutes. Add the onion and bell pepper, season with salt and pepper and cook, scraping up the browned bits, until the vegetables soften, about 4 minutes. Add the marinara sauce, bring to a simmer and cook 5 minutes. Remove from the heat and stir in the cooked mushrooms, ham, olives and ¾ cup pepperoni; season with salt and pepper. Let cool slightly.

2. Meanwhile, preheat the oven to 375˚. Brush an 8-inch round springform pan with olive oil and line with foil, leaving an overhang. Bring a pot of salted water to a boil. Add the noodles and cook as the label directs; drain and toss with the remaining 1 tablespoon olive oil.

3. Combine 2 cups mozzarella, the ricotta, parmesan and eggs in a bowl; season with ½ teaspoon salt and a few grinds of pepper.

4. Wrap some lasagna noodles around the inside of the pan, overlapping slightly and trimming as needed. Cover the bottom of the pan with more noodles, overlapping slightly and letting them extend up the side of the pan. Spread 2 cups sausage sauce in the pan and top with half of the ricotta mixture; cover with a layer of noodles. Repeat with 2 more cups sauce, the remaining ricotta mixture and another layer of noodles, letting them extend up the side of the pan (you might not use all the noodles). Top with the remaining sauce, 1 cup mozzarella and ¼ cup pepperoni.

5. Bake until browned and bubbling, about 1 hour. Let stand 30 minutes to 1 hour, then lift out of the pan using the foil. Remove the foil.

Barbecue Sausage French Bread Pizzas

ACTIVE: 35 min **|** TOTAL: 45 min **|** SERVES: 8

1   24-inch loaf soft French or
    Italian bread
¼   cup extra-virgin olive oil
2   cloves garlic, grated
½   teaspoon dried oregano
Kosher salt and freshly ground
    pepper
6   ounces smoked sausage,
    thinly sliced
1   small onion, thinly sliced
1   green or red bell pepper,
    sliced
½   cup barbecue sauce
2   cups shredded monterey
    jack cheese (about
    8 ounces)
1   cup shredded smoked
    cheddar cheese (about
    4 ounces)
Chopped fresh cilantro,
    for topping

1. Preheat the oven to 500°. Line a rimmed baking sheet with foil. Trim the ends from the bread, then cut into 4 equal pieces; split each piece in half. Arrange the bread, cut-side up, on the prepared baking sheet.

2. Mix 3 tablespoons olive oil with the garlic and oregano. Brush the oil on the cut sides of the bread, then season with salt and pepper. Bake until lightly toasted, 4 to 5 minutes. Let cool slightly.

3. Heat the remaining 1 tablespoon olive oil in a large skillet over medium-high heat. Add the sausage and cook, stirring, until crisp, about 5 minutes. Transfer to a plate with a slotted spoon. Add the onion and bell pepper to the skillet and season with salt and pepper. Cook, stirring occasionally, until tender and lightly browned, about 5 minutes. Stir in ¼ cup barbecue sauce; cook until the vegetables are glazed, about 2 minutes.

4. Combine the monterey jack and cheddar in a medium bowl. Sprinkle about ¼ cup of the cheese mixture onto each bread slice, then top with the onion-pepper mixture, sausage and remaining cheese. Bake until the cheese is melted and bubbling, about 8 minutes.

5. Microwave the remaining ¼ cup barbecue sauce in a microwave-safe bowl until warm, about 30 seconds. Drizzle on the pizzas and sprinkle with cilantro.

PRO TIPS

Soft loaves are best for French bread pizza. Crusty bread may be too chewy.

Don't wipe out the pan after you fry the sausage: Cook the onion and bell pepper in the drippings.

When topping a pizza like this one with two kinds of cheese, pre-mix them; you'll get a more even blend.

This topping tastes
like spinach–
artichoke dip!

Spinach-Artichoke Pizza Bagels

ACTIVE: 25 min **I** TOTAL: 40 min **I** SERVES: 6

1   10-ounce box frozen
     chopped spinach, thawed
     and squeezed dry
1   10-ounce box frozen
     artichoke hearts, thawed
     and squeezed dry
1   8-ounce package cream
     cheese, at room
     temperature
½   cup grated parmesan
     cheese, plus more for
     topping
⅓   cup mayonnaise
⅓   cup sour cream
2   cloves garlic, grated
1   teaspoon grated lemon
     zest
Kosher salt and freshly ground
     pepper
6   plain or sesame bagels, split
1   cup whole-milk ricotta
     cheese
2   cups shredded mozzarella
     cheese (about 8 ounces)
Red pepper flakes, for topping

1. Preheat the oven to 500°. Combine the spinach, artichokes, cream cheese, parmesan, mayonnaise, sour cream, garlic, lemon zest, ½ teaspoon salt and a few grinds of pepper in a food processor. Puree until very smooth.

2. Put the bagels, cut-side up, on a rimmed baking sheet. Bake until lightly toasted, about 5 minutes. Spread a heaping ¼ cup of the spinach mixture on each bagel half. Dot each with 3 small spoonfuls of ricotta, then sprinkle with mozzarella. Bake until the cheese is melted and bubbling, 10 to 12 minutes.

3. Top the pizza bagels with more parmesan and a pinch of red pepper flakes.

PRO TIPS

Frozen spinach and artichokes contain a lot of moisture. Let them thaw, then wring dry in a kitchen towel before using.

Use a fine grater (such as a Microplane) to grate garlic for pizza. You'll get superfine pieces and tons of great garlic flavor.

Philly Cheesesteak Pita Pizzas

ACTIVE: 25 min **I** TOTAL: 25 min **I** SERVES: 4

3	tablespoons extra-virgin olive oil
1	small onion, halved and thinly sliced
1	Italian frying pepper, thinly sliced
1	clove garlic, minced
1	pound shaved or very thinly sliced beef
¼	cup chopped fresh parsley

Kosher salt and freshly ground pepper

4	whole-wheat pocketless pitas
2	cups shredded Italian cheese blend
½	cup pickled sliced sweet or hot cherry peppers

1. Preheat the broiler. Heat the olive oil in a large nonstick skillet over medium-high heat. Add the onion and frying pepper and cook, stirring occasionally, until slightly softened, about 5 minutes. Add the garlic and beef and cook, stirring occasionally, until the beef begins to brown, about 3 minutes. Add the parsley, ¾ teaspoon salt and ½ teaspoon pepper and cook, stirring, 1 more minute.

2. Meanwhile, line a baking sheet with foil. Place the pitas on the prepared baking sheet and sprinkle each with ¼ cup cheese. Top evenly with the beef mixture and the remaining 1 cup cheese.

3. Broil the pizzas until the cheese melts, about 2 minutes. Top with the cherry peppers.

PRO TIPS

Italian frying peppers are long, thin and sweet. Cubanelles and banana peppers are two common varieties.

Shaved beef is steak that's sold very thinly sliced. If you can't find it, freeze a regular steak for about 10 minutes, then slice as thin as possible.

Pre-cooked beets are a real time saver!

Beet and Onion Pie

ACTIVE: 30 min **I** TOTAL: 40 min **I** SERVES: 4

2   8.8-ounce packages fully cooked beets, cut into ⅛- to ¼-inch-thick rounds

1½   teaspoons fresh thyme, chopped

3   tablespoons extra-virgin olive oil, plus more for brushing

Kosher salt

1   round refrigerated pie dough (half of a 14-ounce package)

All-purpose flour, for dusting

4   ounces soft garlic-and-herb cheese (such as Boursin)

1   small onion, thinly sliced

2   tablespoons balsamic vinegar

2   tablespoons chopped walnuts

1   tablespoon finely chopped chives

4   cups mesclun greens

1. Preheat the oven to 425°. Pat the beets very dry with paper towels. Toss in a large bowl with the thyme, 1 tablespoon olive oil and ½ teaspoon salt.

2. Roll out the pie dough on a lightly floured surface into a 13-inch round; place on an inverted baking sheet. Spread the cheese evenly on the dough, leaving a 1½-inch border. Shingle the beet rounds over the cheese. Fold in the edge of the dough over the beets, pleating as needed. Lightly brush the dough with olive oil. Bake until the edge and bottom are golden brown, 25 to 30 minutes.

3. Meanwhile, heat 1 tablespoon olive oil in a small skillet over medium heat. Add the onion, season with salt and cook, tossing occasionally, until golden and caramelized, about 15 minutes. Add 1 tablespoon balsamic vinegar and cook until the liquid is absorbed, 1 more minute.

4. Top the pie with the caramelized onion, walnuts and chives. Whisk the remaining 1 tablespoon balsamic vinegar and 1 tablespoon olive oil in a large bowl. Add the greens, season with salt and gently toss. Serve with the pie.

PRO TIPS

To prevent leaking, be sure to drain the beets, then slice them and pat them very dry.

Garlic-and-herb cheese is great for shortcut pizzas—it's soft enough to spread and it's packed with flavor.

Artichoke French Bread Pizzas

ACTIVE: 10 min ▎ TOTAL: 20 min ▎ SERVES: 2 to 4

¼ cup extra-virgin olive oil
1 clove garlic, minced
½ teaspoon red pepper flakes
½ teaspoon dried oregano
Kosher salt
1 small soft baguette,
split in half lengthwise
½ cup ricotta cheese
½ cup chopped marinated
artichoke hearts
½ cup shredded mozzarella
cheese
Chopped fresh parsley,
for sprinkling

1. Preheat the broiler. Combine the olive oil, garlic, red pepper flakes, oregano and ½ teaspoon salt in a small bowl. Brush onto the cut sides of the baguette.

2. Place the baguette halves on a baking sheet. Top with the ricotta, artichoke hearts and mozzarella. Broil until the cheese is browned and bubbling, about 10 minutes. Top with parsley.

Naan Pizzas with Tandoori Chicken

ACTIVE: 40 min I TOTAL: 40 min I SERVES: 4

1   cup plain whole-milk yogurt

3   tablespoons jarred tandoori paste or marinade

1   pound thin skinless, boneless chicken breasts

Kosher salt and freshly ground pepper

½   English cucumber, grated on the large holes of a box grater

1   tablespoon unsalted butter, at room temperature

4   pieces naan

¼   teaspoon garam masala

½   cup packed fresh cilantro and/or mint, roughly chopped, plus more for topping

Juice of ¼ lemon

4   ounces paneer, halloumi or feta cheese, cut into small pieces

¼   red onion, thinly sliced

1. Preheat the broiler. Line 2 baking sheets with foil. Combine ¼ cup yogurt with the tandoori paste in a medium bowl. Add the chicken, season with salt and pepper and toss well. Set aside for 10 minutes. Toss the grated cucumber with ¼ teaspoon salt in a colander; set aside to drain.

2. Butter the naan on one side and sprinkle with the garam masala. Place on one of the baking sheets and broil until lightly toasted, about 2 minutes. Arrange the chicken on the other baking sheet and broil until cooked through and starting to brown, about 8 minutes. Transfer to a cutting board and let cool, then chop.

3. While the chicken cooks, squeeze the cucumber with your hands to remove the excess moisture. Mix the cucumber with the herbs, lemon juice, remaining ¾ cup yogurt and 1 tablespoon water; season with salt and pepper.

4. Scatter the chicken, cheese and red onion evenly over the naan. Broil until the naan is lightly browned and the cheese softens, 1 to 2 minutes. Spoon the cucumber yogurt over the pizzas. Top with more herbs.

Naan is the perfect size for individual pizzas.

Beef Pita Pizzas

ACTIVE: 30 min | TOTAL: 35 min | SERVES: 4

3   tablespoons extra-virgin olive oil
1   medium onion, finely chopped
1   medium red bell pepper, finely chopped
2   tablespoons tomato paste
8   ounces 90% lean ground beef
Kosher salt and freshly ground pepper
½   cup plain 2% Greek yogurt
1   tablespoon plus 2 teaspoons red wine vinegar
4   whole-wheat pocketless pitas
1   head green-leaf lettuce, torn into pieces
½   cup pickled beets, cut into bite-size pieces
1   small cucumber, peeled and cut into half moons

1. Position a rack in the upper third of the oven and preheat to 400°. Heat 1 tablespoon olive oil in a large nonstick skillet over medium-high heat. Add the onion and bell pepper and cook, stirring occasionally, until golden, 6 to 8 minutes. Add the tomato paste and cook, stirring, until brick red, 1 minute. Add the beef, 2 tablespoons water, ¾ teaspoon salt, and pepper to taste and cook, breaking up the meat, until browned, 3 to 4 minutes. Remove from the heat and stir in ¼ cup yogurt and 2 teaspoons vinegar. Season with salt and pepper and transfer to a bowl.

2. Wipe out the skillet and return to medium heat. Brush the pitas with 1 tablespoon olive oil, then lightly toast in the skillet, about 45 seconds per side. Arrange the pitas on a baking sheet and top evenly with the beef mixture. Transfer to the oven and bake 6 minutes.

3. Whisk the remaining ¼ cup yogurt, 1 tablespoon each olive oil and vinegar, and salt and pepper to taste in a bowl. Add the lettuce, beets and cucumber and toss. Serve the pizzas with the salad.

PRO TIPS

Toast the pitas briefly in a skillet before topping so they stay crispy even after you add the beef.

If you have extra Greek yogurt, thin it out with a little water and drizzle it on top of your finished pizza.

Think of this as
the sloppy joe
of pizzas!

A

All-Purpose Pizza Dough, 15
All-Purpose Pizza Sauce, 16
Alternative pizzas, 133–171. *See also*
French bread pizzas; Pita pizzas; Puff
pastry pizzas; Tortilla pizzas
  about: overview and photos of, 12
  Beet and Onion Pie, 167
  Cauliflower-Crust Pizzas with
    Artichokes, 155
  Cauliflower-Crust Pizza with
    Mushrooms, 148–149
  Ham and Cheese Pie with
    Artichokes and Broccoli, 136–137
  Jalapeño Popper Tortilla Pizzas, 151
  Lavash Pizzas with Arugula and
    Prosciutto, 140–141
  Naan Pizzas with Tandoori
    Chicken, 169
  Pepperoni Pizzagna, 159
  Spinach-Artichoke Pizza Bagels, 163
Artichokes
  about: frozen, 163
  Artichoke French Bread Pizzas, 168
  Cauliflower-Crust Pizzas with
    Artichokes, 155
  Grilled Pizza with Eggplant and
    Artichokes, 131
  Ham and Cheese Pie with
    Artichokes and Broccoli, 136–137
  Quattro Stagioni Pizzas, 71
  Spinach-Artichoke Pizza Bagels, 163
Arugula
  Sheet-Pan Pizza with Arugula
    Pesto, 94–95
  Arugula-Prosciutto Pizza, 63
  Grilled Pita Pizzas with Tomatoes,
    Olives and Arugula, 156–157
  Individual Mushroom Pizzas with
    Arugula, 42–43
  Lavash Pizzas with Arugula and
    Prosciutto, 140–141
  Sausage Pizza with Arugula and
    Grapes, 68–69
Asparagus-Beet Puff Pastry Pizza,
  152–153

B

Bacon and pancetta
  about: Canadian bacon, 106; dicing
    raw bacon, 67
  Bacon-and-Egg Puff Pastry Pizzas,
    143
  Brussels Sprouts–Pancetta Pizza,
    60
  Grilled Ranch Pizza with Bacon and
    Broccoli, 129
  Grilled White Pizza with Fennel
    Salad, 115
  Jalapeño Popper Tortilla Pizzas, 151
  Mini Bacon-and-Egg Pizzas, 61
  Potato and Bacon Pizza, 67
  Sheet-Pan Hawaiian Pizza, 106–107
  Three-Cheese Bacon Pizzas, 45
Bagels
  Everything Bagel Pizza, 76–77
  Spinach-Artichoke Pizza Bagels, 163
Baking steel, 16
Barbecue Chicken Pizza, 34–35
Barbecue Mushroom Pizza, 72–73
Barbecue Sausage French Bread
  Pizzas, 160–161
Basic Deep-Dish Pizzas, 101
Basic Pizzas with Homemade Sauce,
  29
Basic Sicilian Pizza, 89
Basic Thin-Crust Pizzas, 21
Beans
  Grilled Pizza with Hummus and
    Tomatoes, 121
  Tortilla Pizzas with Chorizo, 144–145
  Taco Pizza, 79
Beef
  about: slicing thinly, 164
  Beef Pita Pizzas, 170–171
  Corned Beef and Cabbage Pizzas,
    83
  Meatball Pizza, 46–47
  Philly Cheesesteak Pita Pizzas,
    164–165
  Skillet Taco Pizza, 97
Beets
  Asparagus-Beet Puff Pastry Pizza,
    152–153

Beet and Onion Pie, 167
Broccoli, broccolini, and broccoli rabe
  about: adding as toppings, 76;
    broccolini vs. broccoli rabe, 80
  Grilled Ranch Pizza with Bacon
    and Broccoli, 129
  Ham and Cheese Pie with
    Artichokes and Broccoli, 136–137
  Pizza with Clams and Broccoli
    Rabe, 64–65
  Sausage and Broccolini Pizza, 33
  White Pizza with Broccolini,
    80–81
Brussels Sprouts–Pancetta Pizza, 60
Butternut Squash–Soppressata Pizza,
  55

C

Cabbage, in Corned Beef and Cabbage
  Pizzas, 83
Cacio e Pepe Pizza with Ricotta, 52–53
Carrots, in Tahini-Carrot Puff Pastry
  Pizza, 135
Cauliflower
  Cauliflower-Crust Pizzas with
    Artichokes, 155
  Cauliflower-Crust Pizza with
    Mushrooms, 148–149
  Cauliflower, Tomato and Olive
    Pizza, 59
Cheese. *See also specific recipes*
  about: Cambozola, 67; garlic-and-
    herb, 167
  burrata, pizza with, 128
  feta, pizzas with, 121, 123, 126–127,
    169
  fontina, pizzas with, 120, 140
  gorgonzola, pizza with, 140–141
  gruyère, pizza with, 120, 136–137
  halloumi, pizzas with, 169
  keeping from over-browning, 99
  Tortilla Pizzas with Chorizo 144–145
  paneer, pizzas with, 169
  under sauce, 99
  seasoning ricotta, 68
  shaving hard cheeses, 63

Cheesesteak pita pizzas, 164–165
Chicken
    Barbecue Chicken Pizza, 34–35
    Naan Pizzas with Tandoori
        Chicken, 169
Chorizo. *See* Sausage
Clams. *See* Seafood
Corn, grilled pizza with spicy chorizo
    and, 124
Cornmeal, uses, 63, 100

Deep-dish pizza. *See* Pan pizzas
Dough. *See also specific recipes*
    about: baking with ice on top,
        52; buying from pizzerias, 79;
        freezing, 49; preventing from
        sticking to peel, 63; store-bought,
        dressing up, 37; stretching, 76;
        tips for making, storing, 15, 22, 52
    All-Purpose Pizza Dough, 15
    alternatives to traditional.
        See Alternative pizzas

E

Eggplant, grilled pizza with artichokes
    and, 131
Eggs
    Bacon-and-Egg Puff Pastry Pizzas,
        143
    Mini Bacon-and-Egg Pizzas, 61
Everything Bagel Pizza, 76–77

F

Fennel
    Grilled White Pizza with Fennel
        Salad, 115
    Sheet-Pan Pizza with Potatoes and
        Fennel, 86–87
Freezing
    bacon, for dicing, 67
    beef, to thinly slice, 164
    dough, 49
    pizza, 100
    sauce, 28

French bread pizzas
    Artichoke French Bread Pizzas, 168
    Barbecue Sausage French Bread
        Pizzas, 160–161

G

Garlic
    about: dressing up store-bought
        dough with garlic oil, 37;
        garlic-and-herb cheese, 167;
        grating, 163
    Grilled White Pizza with Garlic, 125
Grapes, sausage pizza with arugula
    and, 68–69
Greens. *See* Arugula; Spinach
Grilled pizzas, 113–131
    about: hot spots on grills, 125;
        overview and photos of, 11; rustic
        shapes for, 115
    Grilled Pita Pizzas with Tomatoes,
        Olives and Arugula, 156–157
    Grilled Pizza alla Vodka, 116
    Grilled Pizza with Eggplant and
        Artichokes, 131
    Grilled Pizza with Hummus and
        Tomatoes, 121
    Grilled Pizza with Mushrooms and
        Fontina, 120
    Grilled Pizza with Peaches and
        Burrata, 128
    Grilled Pizza with Pork and
        Pineapple, 118–119
    Grilled Pizza with Shrimp and Feta,
        123
    Grilled Pizza with Spicy Chorizo
        and Corn, 124
    Grilled Pizza with Spinach and
        Kale, 117
    Grilled Pizza with Summer Squash,
        126–127
    Grilled Ranch Pizza with Bacon and
        Broccoli, 129
    Grilled White Pizza with Fennel
        Salad, 115
    Grilled White Pizza with Garlic, 125

H

Ham/prosciutto
    about: Canadian bacon and, 106
    Arugula-Prosciutto Pizza, 63
    Ham and Cheese Pie with
        Artichokes and Broccoli, 136–137
    Hawaiian Pizza with Grilled
        Pineapple, 26–27
    Lavash Pizzas with Arugula and
        Prosciutto, 140–141
    Quattro Stagioni Pizzas, 71
Hawaiian Pizza with Grilled Pineapple,
    26–27. *See also* Sheet-Pan Hawaiian
    Pizza
Heirloom Tomato Puff Pastry Pizza,
    147
Honey (hot), sheet-pan pepperoni
    pizza with, 105
Hummus, grilled pizza with, 121

I

Individual Mushroom Pizzas with
    Arugula, 42–43

K

Kale, grilled pizza with spinach and,
    117

L

Lavash Pizzas with Arugula and
    Prosciutto, 140–141

M

Making pizza, 14–17
    All-Purpose Pizza Dough, 15
    basic guidelines, 15
    cooling before slicing, 17
    tools for, 16
    topping tips, 16
Margherita Pizzas, 25. *See also* Spicy
    Margherita Pizzas
Meatball Pizza, 46–47

Meatless pizzas
    Artichoke French Bread Pizzas, 168
    Sheet-Pan Pizza with Arugula
      Pesto, 94-95
    Asparagus-Beet Puff Pastry Pizza,
      152-153
    Barbecue Mushroom Pizza, 72-73
    Basic Deep-Dish Pizzas, 101
    Basic Pizzas with Homemade
      Sauce, 29
    Basic Sicilian Pizza, 89
    Basic Thin-Crust Pizzas, 21
    Beet and Onion Pie, 167
    Butternut Squash-Soppressata
      Pizza, 55
    Cacio e Pepe Pizza with Ricotta,
      52-53
    Cauliflower-Crust Pizza with
      Mushrooms, 148-149
    Cauliflower, Tomato and
      Olive Pizza, 59
    Everything Bagel Pizza, 76-77
    Grilled Pita Pizzas with Tomatoes,
      Olives and Arugula, 156-157
    Grilled Pizza alla Vodka, 116
    Grilled Pizza with Eggplant and
      Artichokes, 131
    Grilled Pizza with Hummus and
      Tomatoes, 121
    Grilled Pizza with Mushrooms and
      Fontina, 120
    Grilled Pizza with Peaches and
      Burrata, 128
    Grilled Pizza with Spinach and
      Kale, 117
    Grilled Pizza with Summer Squash,
      126-127
    Heirloom Tomato Puff Pastry Pizza,
      147
    Individual Mushroom Pizzas with
      Arugula, 42-43
    Margherita Pizzas, 25
    Neapolitan Pizzas, 22-23
    New York-Style Pizza, 38-39
    Potato-Rosemary Pizza, 56-57
    Sheet-Pan Pizza alla Vodka, 93
    Sheet-Pan Pizza with Potatoes and
      Fennel, 86-87
    Sheet-Pan Pizza with Roasted Red
      Peppers, 109
    Sheet-Pan Spinach Pizza with
      Sesame Seeds, 110-111
    Spicy Margherita Pizzas, 49
    Spinach-Artichoke Pizza Bagels, 163
    Taco Pizza, 79
    Tahini-Carrot Puff Pastry Pizza, 135
    Thin-Crust Veggie Pizzas, 30-31
    Three-Cheese White Pizzas, 41
    Grilled White Pizza with Garlic, 125
    White Pizza with Broccolini, 80-81
Meats. *See* specific meats
Mushrooms
    about: cleaning, 71
    Barbecue Mushroom Pizza, 72-73
    Cauliflower-Crust Pizza with
      Mushrooms, 148-149
    Grilled Pizza with Mushrooms and
      Fontina, 120
    Individual Mushroom Pizzas with
      Arugula, 42-43
    Pepperoni Pizzagna with, 159
    Quattro Stagioni Pizzas, 71
    Thin-Crust Veggie Pizzas, 30-31

Naan Pizzas with Tandoori Chicken,
  169
New York-Style Pizza, 38-39

Olives
    about: pitting, 59
    Cauliflower, Tomato and Olive
      Pizza, 59
    Deep-Dish Pizza with Spicy
      Sausage and Olives, 98-99
    Grilled Pita Pizzas with Tomatoes,
      Olives and Arugula, 156-157
    Quattro Stagioni Pizzas, 71
Onions
    about: caramelizing, 152; grilling,
      123; shallots and, 68
    Beet and Onion Pie, 167

Pancetta. *See* Bacon and pancetta
Pan pizzas, 85-111
    about: dark metal pans for, 102;
      overview and photos of, 10;
      sheet pan for, 16; using stone
      with, 46
    Sheet-Pan Pizza with Arugula
      Pesto, 94-95
    Basic Deep-Dish Pizzas, 101
    Basic Sicilian Pizza, 89
    Deep-Dish Pepperoni Pizza with
      Pepperoncini, 102-103
    Deep-Dish Pizza with Spicy
      Sausage and Olives, 98-99
    Sheet-Pan Hawaiian Pizza, 106-107
    Sheet-Pan Pepperoni Pizza with
      Hot Honey, 105
    Sheet-Pan Pizza alla Vodka, 93
    Sheet-Pan Pizza with Potatoes and
      Fennel, 86-87
    Sheet-Pan Pizza with Roasted Red
      Peppers, 109
    Sheet-Pan Spinach Pizza with
      Sesame Seeds, 110-111
    Sicilian Pizza with Sausage and
      Peppers, 90-91
    Skillet Taco Pizza, 97
Peaches, grilled pizza with burrata
  and, 128
Peel, pizza, 16
Pepperoni
    Deep-Dish Pepperoni Pizza with
      Pepperoncini, 102-103
    Pepperoni Pizzagna, 159
    Sheet-Pan Pepperoni Pizza with
      Hot Honey, 105
Pepper(s)
    about: using jalapeño brine, 34
    Cacio e Pepe Pizza with Ricotta,
      52-53
    Deep-Dish Pepperoni Pizza with
      Pepperoncini, 102-103
    Jalapeño Popper Tortilla Pizzas,
      151
    Sheet-Pan Pizza with Roasted Red
      Peppers, 109

Sicilian Pizza with Sausage and Peppers, 90–91

Thin-Crust Veggie Pizzas, 30–31

Pesto, in Sheet-Pan Pizza with Arugula Pesto, 94–95. See also Grilled Pizza with Spinach and Kale

Philly Cheesesteak Pita Pizzas, 164–165

Pineapple
  about: peeling, 26
  Grilled Pizza with Pork and Pineapple, 118–119
  Hawaiian Pizza with Grilled Pineapple, 26–27
  Sheet-Pan Hawaiian Pizza, 106–107

Pita pizzas
  about: pocketless pitas for, 156
  Beef Pita Pizzas, 170–171
  Grilled Pita Pizzas with Tomatoes, Olives and Arugula, 156–157
  Philly Cheesesteak Pita Pizzas, 164–165

Pizza peel, 16

Pizza stone, 16

Pizza with Clams and Broccoli Rabe, 64–65

Pork. See also Bacon and pancetta; Ham/prosciutto; Pepperoni
  Grilled Pizza with Pork and Pineapple, 118–119
  Meatball Pizza, 46–47

Potatoes
  Corned Beef and Cabbage Pizzas, 83
  Potato and Bacon Pizza, 67
  Potato-Rosemary Pizza, 56–57
  Sheet-Pan Pizza with Potatoes and Fennel, 86–87

Prosciutto. See Ham/prosciutto

Puff pastry pizzas
  about: creating raised edges, 147; thawing puff pastry, 135; working with puff pastry, 135
  Asparagus-Beet Puff Pastry Pizza, 152–153
  Bacon-and-Egg Puff Pastry Pizzas, 143

Heirloom Tomato Puff Pastry Pizza, 147

Smoked Salmon Puff Pastry Pizza, 139

Tahini-Carrot Puff Pastry Pizza, 135

Q

Quattro Stagioni Pizzas, 71

R

Rosemary, in other pizzas, 63, 156–157

Rosemary, in Potato-Rosemary Pizza, 56–57

S

Salmon, in Smoked Salmon Puff Pastry Pizza, 139

Sauce. See also specific recipes
  about: doctoring up store-bought, 45; storing, 28
  All-Purpose Pizza Sauce, 16

Sausage. See also Pepperoni
  Barbecue Sausage French Bread Pizzas, 160–161
  Deep-Dish Pizza with Spicy Sausage and Olives, 98–99
  Grilled Pizza with Spicy Chorizo and Corn, 124
  Sausage and Broccolini Pizza, 33
  Sausage Pizza with Arugula and Grapes, 68–69
  Sausage Pizza with Spinach Salad, 75
  Sicilian Pizza with Sausage and Peppers, 90–91
  Tortilla Pizzas with Chorizo, 144–145

Seafood
  Grilled Pizza with Shrimp and Feta, 123
  Pizza with Clams and Broccoli Rabe, 64–65
  Smoked Salmon Puff Pastry Pizza, 139
  White Clam Pizza, 37

Sesame seeds, sheet-pan spinach pizza with, 110–111

Sheet-pan pizza. See Pan pizzas

Shrimp, grilled pizza with feta and, 123

Sicilian Pizza with Sausage and Peppers, 90–91. See also Basic Sicilian Pizza

Simple pizzas, 19–49
  about: overview and photos of, 8
  Barbecue Chicken Pizza, 34–35
  Basic Pizzas with Homemade Sauce, 29
  Basic Thin-Crust Pizzas, 21
  Hawaiian Pizza with Grilled Pineapple, 26–27
  Individual Mushroom Pizzas with Arugula, 42–43
  Margherita Pizzas, 25
  Meatball Pizza, 46–47
  Neapolitan Pizzas, 22–23
  New York–Style Pizza, 38–39
  Sausage and Broccolini Pizza, 33
  Spicy Margherita Pizzas, 49
  Thin-Crust Veggie Pizzas, 30–31
  Three-Cheese Bacon Pizzas, 45
  Three-Cheese White Pizzas, 41
  White Clam Pizza, 37

Skillet Taco Pizza, 97

Slicing pizza, tip, 17

Smoked Salmon Puff Pastry Pizza, 139

Soppressata Pizza, 55

Specialty pizzas, 51–83
  about: overview and photos of, 9
  Arugula-Prosciutto Pizza, 63
  Barbecue Mushroom Pizza, 72–73
  Brussels Sprouts–Pancetta Pizza, 60
  Butternut Squash–Soppressata Pizza, 55
  Cacio e Pepe Pizza with Ricotta, 52–53
  Cauliflower, Tomato and Olive Pizza, 59
  Corned Beef and Cabbage Pizzas, 83
  Everything Bagel Pizza, 76–77

Mini Bacon-and-Egg Pizzas, 61
Pizza with Clams and Broccoli
Rabe, 64–65
Potato and Bacon Pizza, 67
Potato-Rosemary Pizza, 56–57
Quattro Stagioni Pizzas, 71
Sausage Pizza with Arugula and
Grapes, 68–69
Sausage Pizza with Spinach Salad,
. 75
Taco Pizza, 79
White Pizza with Broccolini, 80–81
Spicy Margherita Pizzas, 49
Spinach
about: frozen, 163
Grilled Pizza with Spinach and
Kale, 117
Sausage Pizza with Spinach Salad,
75
Sheet-Pan Spinach Pizza with
Sesame Seeds, 110–111
Spinach-Artichoke Pizza Bagels,
163
Squash
Sheet-Pan Pizza with Arugula
Pesto, 94–95
Butternut Squash–Soppressata
Pizza, 55
Grilled Pizza with Summer Squash,
126–127
Steel, baking on, 16
Stone, pizza, 16

T

Taco Pizza, 79. See also Skillet Taco
Pizza
Tahini-Carrot Puff Pastry Pizza, 135
Thin-crust pizzas, basic, 21
Thin-Crust Veggie Pizzas, 30–31
Three-Cheese White Pizzas, 41
Tomatoes
about: draining canned, 33; from
Italy, 89
All-Purpose Pizza Sauce, 16
Cauliflower, Tomato and Olive
Pizza, 59

Grilled Pita Pizzas with Tomatoes,
Olives and Arugula, 156–157
Grilled Pizza with Hummus and
Tomatoes, 121
Heirloom Tomato Puff Pastry Pizza,
147
Toppings, tips for, 16, 24, 28. See also
specific toppings
Tortilla pizzas
Jalapeño Popper Tortilla Pizzas, 151
Tortilla Pizzas with Chorizo,
144–145

V

Vodka
Grilled Pizza alla Vodka, 116
Sheet-Pan Pizza alla Vodka, 93

W

White pizzas
Grilled White Pizza with Fennel
Salad, 115
Three-Cheese White Pizzas, 41
White Clam Pizza, 37
Grilled White Pizza with Garlic, 125
White Pizza with Broccolini,
80–81

Z

Zucchini, pizzas with, 94–95, 126–127